THE KEY
TO HOYLE'S
GAMES

THE KEY
TO HOYLE'S
GAMES

WESTPORT
PUBLISHERS
FAIRFIELD N.J 07006

TABLE OF CONTENTS

CONTENTS

CONTENTS

CONTENTS

BLACKJACK

Blackjack is known also as Twenty-one. Blackjack is a group game which has been adapted to casino play, where it has become extremely popular. In Blackjack, a 52-card pack is used, but suits are disregarded. An Ace is valued at either 1 or 11, as the person holding it prefers; picture cards, Kings, Queens, Jacks, are valued at 10 each. Other cards are given their face values; Ten:10, Nine:9, Eight:8 and so on down to Two:2.

In the group game, ten or even more players may participate. The dealer, who has a special advantage, deals a card face down to each player, including himself. Each player may look at his card, and then make a bet, from a required minimum, say, one unit, up to a limit, which is previously set, as 10 units. The dealer does not bet.

Each player, including the dealer, is then dealt another card face up, so he has a hole card and an upcard. The immediate aim is to make a total of 21—Ace:11, plus a *tenth* card:10, or vice versa. This strongly influences each player's bet, as he is apt to go the limit with an Ace as the downcard.

If the dealer hits a *natural 21*, as this is termed, he shows his hole card and he wins double from each player, unless a player also has a natural 21. Then, the dealer wins whatever was bet by that player, no more. However, if a player hits a natural 21, and the dealer does not, the player is paid double.

When the dealer fails to hit a natural 21, each player, in turn, may call for as many face up cards as he wants. Now, a player wants to come as close to 21 as possible, without going over. If his two cards total less than 11, he will call for more, one by one; but as soon as he is above 11, he may prefer to stand on what he has.

Holding a Two and Four, total 6, a player would take a card. A Three would make his total 9, so he would call for another. A King would make his total 19, and he would stand. But if he received a Six, his total—2, 4, 3, 6—would be only 15, raising the question, could that beat the dealer? His course of play would be determined by the upcard held by the dealer. If the dealer's card is low, the player may decide to stay—hoping that the dealer would go bust in the draw. However, if the dealer's upcard is high, then the player would be apt to call for another card, even at the risk of going over 21.

When a player *goes bust* with a total of more than 21, the dealer takes in his bet. But players who stand with anything up to 21, simply wait for the dealer to add face up cards to his own. If the dealer stands with less than 21, say with Two, Eight, Nine, total 19, he collects from all players having that amount or less, so in case of ties, the dealer wins, that being his advantage.

But any player with a higher total than the dealer's collects from him, according to the amount of the bets; and if the dealer goes bust with a total exceeding 21, he must pay to all the players who stood. Here, however, the dealer still has the edge, since, as the game progresses, he collects immediately from any player who goes bust, before he personally goes bust.

In Blackjack, a dealer keeps the deal until some player hits a natural 21 without the dealer matching it. The dealing privilege then goes to that player. At the start of the game, cards are dealt around and the first person receiving an Ace, gets the deal. Before any hand, the dealer can sell the dealing privilege to the highest bidder among the other players.

Doubling the bet is another privilege granted to the dealer. After looking at his hole card, he can wait until all bets have been made; then demand that they be doubled, giving him a chance to win as much as if he held a natural 21. The dealer often does this when both his hole card and upcards are tenths, giving him a standing total of 20.

Players, in contrast, have the privilege of *splitting pairs* before calling for cards. Assume that a player has been dealt two Tens, one down, one up. On his turn to call for cards, he turns the downcard face up, announcing that he is splitting pairs, treating each as an upcard. He duplicates his original bet, placing it on the second card. He is then dealt a downcard to go with each of the upcards.

Thus he is playing two hands, in turn. He calls for other cards, or decides to stand with one; then does the same with the other. It is usually agreed that if a player hits 21 on his new downcard, it is not regarded as a natural because it was not actually made on the first two cards dealt to him.

In gambling houses, the game is often limited to six or seven players, with no change of dealer, as the house provides its own. The dealer begins by turning a card face up and placing it on the bottom of the pack as a marker. This is called *burning a card*. A deal follows and bets are made and paid; the dealer gathers up each player's cards and puts them face up beneath the pack.

Dealing continues until the burnt card is approached or reached. The pack is then reshuffled, another card burnt, and the deal proceeds. Two or more packs may be combined as one, bringing up fresh cards constantly. This may be applied in private games. Other factors, however, are more important in the house games.

Players are dealt both cards face down; dealer, one down, one up, as usual. Players demand cards or stand as they choose, but the dealer must follow a set rule. With a total of 17 or above, he must stand; below 17, he must take a card. This applies even if he holds an Ace, as long as it can be safely counted as 11.

Thus a player holding an Ace, Seven, could count the Ace as 1, total 8, and could safely call for another card. If he should catch a Two or Three, he could term the Ace as 11, and stand on 20 or 21 as the case might be. If instead, he caught a Ten or above, he could term the Ace as 1, and his total—1, 7, 10—would enable him to stand on 18.

But the dealer, holding an Ace, Six would have to count the Ace as 11, and would be forced to stand on 17. Often, too, if a dealer has a Seven, Eight or Nine as upcard, a player can chance it that the dealer's downcard is a tenth, which will force the dealer to stand on 17, 18, 19. This helps the player decide whether to call for a card or stand.

In some games, the dealer must draw on an Ace and Six, 17, and must stand on an Ace and Seven, 18, or higher. This is helpful to the dealer. In other games, players are dealt their first two cards face up instead of face down, so they may compare holdings. This helps the players, but not the dealer whose procedure is fixed.

In the casino game, a player is paid 1½ times his bet for a natural 21, but the dealer collects only the amount bet for a natural. On all ties, bets are off. The only advantage for the house is that the dealer collects from each player who goes bust over 21, whether or not the dealer goes bust later. There are no ties on busts.

House rules allow a player to *double down* by doubling his bet after looking at his first two cards, provided he takes one more card and stands. Players may double down after receiving new cards with split pairs. Further splits may be allowed, at the start, so a player receiving three or four cards of the same value, as Kings, may call for a new card with each, to play all as separate hands.

In some casinos, a player may make an *insurance bet* agains the dealer getting a natural 21. There are bonus scores for which some casinos pay set amounts, to a player taking 5, 6, 7, 8, 9 cards, without going bust. A player may receive a bonus for a natural 21 consisting of ♠A, ♠J or for 21 formed by 6, 7, 8 of one suit; or by three Sevens.

House rules vary, and should be carefully checked in advance; they are also subject to frequent change, particularly when new systems are developed to cut into their percentage. So it is best to consider them currently.

Various gambling games follow the style of Blackjack, some quite elaborate and suited to casino play, others adaptable to private groups. Some are given here in simple form, as the more elaborate types may be subject to individual house rules, while those played by groups are easier to follow.

Baccarat or Baccara

Played on a special green felt layout, this game differs from *Vinqt-et-un*, the French term for Twenty-one, alias Blackjack, in the value given to the cards, as well as certain modes of play. Values are Ace:1, Two:2, up to Nine:9, while Tens and picture cards count 0. When two cards are dealt to a player, he adds their values, hoping to make a total of 8 or 9. If the total exceeds 9, the first figure is eliminated.

Thus, 3 and 5 total 8, count as 8; 7 and 6 total 13, count as 3; 9 and 9 total 18, count as 8; K and 10, *O and O*, total 0—though they may be regarded as 10 and 10, total 20, which also counts as 0, so amounts to the same thing.

When a player fails to *hit* 8 or 9 on two cards, he may be dealt a third card, whose value is added to the other two, so

that A, 3, 5 would count as 9; 6, Q, 8 total 14, would count
as 4; 8, 7, 9 total 24, would count as 4.

The original game of Baccarat, which had a permanent
dealer has been largely supplanted by a more modern version
known as *Chemin de Fer*.

Chemin de Fer, Railroad

Also called *Shimmy*, this game is played with a minimum
of three packs, up to six or eight, shuffled together. In gambling casinos, the deal goes from one player to another, with
the house taking a percentage of each pot. The dealer acts as
banker, stating how much he will bet. Beginning at his right,
each player may declare *Banco* and cover the entire amount.
Otherwise different players may take parts of it.

The player making the biggest bet plays for the rest.
Banker deals four cards, face down, alternately, two to the
player and two to himself. If either has a *natural 8 or 9*,
cards are turned up. An 8 beats anything less and a 9 beats
an 8. A tie calls for a new deal.

If neither has a natural, he may either draw another card
or stand on what he has. In casino games, if the player's total
is 0, 1, 2, 3, 4 he must call for another card; with 5, he may
draw or stand; with 6 or 7 he must stand. This is in fairness
to the other players, since he acts as their spokesman.

The player's third card, if any, is dealt face up, giving the
banker a chance to decide if he wants to draw or stand. Originally, this was entirely optional. Today, in casino play, the
banker must also adhere to a set schedule, according to house
rules. The higher count wins; a tie calls for another deal.

In private play, the original rule may still hold; and when a
player declares Banco he, too, may draw a card or stand—as
he prefers, depending upon agreement.

In all forms of Chemin de Fer, the banker must leave his
entire winnings as the next stake, or else give up the deal. If

the full amount is not covered, he may withdraw the rest. However, if he passes the deal, he keeps his full winnings and other players in rotation, may take the deal by putting up that amount. If no one wants it on that basis, the player to the dealer's right becomes banker and can stake whatever he wants.

Dutch Bank

Also known as *Banker and Broker,* this is one of the simplest yet fastest of banking games. One player acts as banker and cuts a shuffled pack into five, six or even more heaps, provided each contains more than four cards. All heaps are face down. More than one player may bet on the same heap of cards. If, after all players have put their stakes on heaps of cards, there is left more than one stack of cards for the dealer, the dealer may choose whichever stack he prefers. For instance: if there are six players, the dealer will lay out six stacks of cards; if five players make their bets on three stacks, the banker may choose any one of the remaining stacks.

All now place limited amounts on whichever heaps they want. The banker then turns the heaps face up, exposing the bottom card of each. Cards are valued Ace, King, Queen down to Two, with suits disregarded.

A player wins if his heap has a card of higher value than the banker's, who pays the amount the player staked. If the banker's card is higher, he collects. In case of a tie, the banker also wins, giving him a decided edge. The deal, in Dutch Bank, passes only when a player hits an Ace. Two methods are used. The deal may pass to the next player on the left. Or, the deal goes to the man who hit the Ace. If more than one player hits an Ace, they choose high card for the deal.

Ferme or Farmer

A distinctive variant of the French Vingt-et-un, based on the idea of leasing out a farm. A 45-card pack is used, all Eights and Sixes being removed, with the exception of the Six of Hearts. Cards are valued Ace:1; Two:2; on up to Ten:10, with picture cards 10 each.

All players contribute a set amount to a pot, so that eight players at 2 units each would be 16 chips. The players then bid for the privilege of working the *farm*, as the pot is called. Whoever bids highest, say 10 chips, becomes the dealer, and gives a face down card to each player, except himself. The auction is added to the pot.

Each player in turn calls for one or more face down cards, looking at each as he receives it, to decide if he wants another or prefers to stand. His purpose is to hit exactly 16 if he can; otherwise to stop short of that total. If he goes over 16, he must stand, but does not reveal that he is over, until all hands are completely dealt, so that all can be turned up at once.

Any player hitting exactly 16 may be the winner of the farm, taking the pot and the deal with it. Preference goes to a 16, which contains the 6♥, as the K♦, 6♥, or 3♠, 5♦, A♥, 6♥, A♣. If no 16 contains the 6♥, the hand with the fewest cards gains preference, so that 7♣, 4♣, 5♦ would win over 9♥, 2♦, A♣, 4♦. If two are tied for a 16, first player to the dealer's left wins.

Any player going over 16, must pay the dealer one unit for each point over. Thus a player holding K♥, J♦ would have 20 points and would pay 4 units. These represent direct profits to the farmer as long as he retains the farm. Even if he loses it to some player who makes 16, he still collects from any others who went over on that deal.

If nobody hits 16, the dealer collects the *overs* and the

player who came nearest to reaching 16 collects one unit from every other player. If two are tied, say at 15, preference is given to one holding the 6♥, then the fewest cards, then first player to the dealer's left, as with a 16. But when no one hits 16 the dealer retains the farm.

Example: A: 5, 7, 2, 4; B: J, Q; C: 5, 6, 3, A; D: 7, A, 7; E: K, 4; F: 10, 3, 4. Since C has the 6♥—the only Six in play—he wins over D and collects 1 unit from each player or 5 in all. The dealer would collect 2 from A, 18; 4 from B, 20; 1 from F, 17.

Macao

Straight from the casinos of Macao, famed gambling center of the Far East, this is a cross between Baccarat and Blackjack. The count resembles Baccarat; Ace:1, Two:2, up to Nine:9, Tens and picture cards:0. But in this game 9 is the limit, as with 21 in Blackjack.

Bets are made before the deal, and a single card is dealt to each player, dealer included, all face down. Sevens, Eights and Nines are naturals and are promptly turned up. A player beating the dealer collects the amount bet on a Seven, twice that on an Eight, three times that on a Nine.

Conversely, the dealer collects triple from each player for a Nine, double for an Eight, the amount bet for a Seven, except in the case of a tie, when individual bets are off, as in Blackjack. If the dealer has no natural, he pays off winners; then the other players draw or stand, aiming to reach 9.

A player going over, loses his stake to the dealer, who then draws or stands, hoping to beat or tie those who stopped at 9 or less. If dealer goes bust, he pays the remaining players; otherwise he settles according to individual scores.

Seven-and-a-Half

Keen card players regard this game as a rival to Blackjack, which it closely resembles, but with a reverse twist. Seven-and-a-Half is played with a 40-card pack, from which all 8's, 9's and 10's have been removed, so that when counting, Ace:1, Two:2, the highest value is Seven:7. The picture cards each have a value of ½ point.

One player serves as dealer, giving a face down card to each player, including himself. Each player's purpose is to reach 7½ without going over, so he is allowed to call for cards, or stand as he pleases. With a Seven as hole card, he has 12 chances out of 39—1 out of 3¼—of hitting a natural Seven-and-a-Half.

In some groups, players bet after receiving the first card; in others, they must bet before. If he hits a natural—Seven with King, Queen or Jack—a player turns it up and wins the amount of his bet, along with the dealing privilege; unless the dealer can match it with another natural, which he too, promptly turns up to collect from everybody.

Otherwise, each player draws or stands, receiving any cards face up. If he goes over 7½, he is busted and pays the dealer; if he reaches 7½ or stops short of it, he wins if the dealer fails to make as high a total or goes bust himself. In games among private groups, a tie is a win for the dealer, as the deal goes to a player hitting a natural, and can also be sold. As a house game, ties are standoffs, as in Blackjack, and the dealer usually pays *double* for a natural, but collects *single* when he gets the natural.

There is a form of 7½ in which the K♦ may be considered either ½ like the other face cards or, a wild card, any whole number from 1 to 7. Thus, K♦ and any other face card is also 7½ — **K♦**: 7, face card: ½. Also a combination of say a Two and a Jack, plus **K♦** is also 7½. In this case the **K♦** is reckoned as a 5.

BRIDGE

This is the most popular of all card games, an outgrowth of Whist, which it follows somewhat in pattern of play. There are four players, commonly known as South, West, North, East, from their positions at the bridge table. Those seated opposite are partners. A pack of 52 cards is used, suits running Ace, King, Queen, down to Two, and it is customary to have two packs available, so the dealer's partner can shuffle one while the other is being dealt. The extra pack is laid to the shuffler's right, to be ready for the next dealer, as the deal rotates to the left.

Cards are dealt singly, as in Whist, but instead of turning up a card for trump, the players, beginning with the dealer, bid for the privilege of naming a trump suit. No-trump is also an allowable bid, signifying a hand in which all suits are equal, with no trump involved.

A bidder and his partner must take at least seven tricks, which is one in excess of a *book*, as six tricks are called in both Whist and Bridge. Since the highest bid stands, suits

18

have a progressive order, beginning with the lowest, of Clubs, Diamonds, Hearts, Spades, No-trump. Thus the smallest bid is One Club, followed by One Diamond, One Heart, One Spade, One No-trump; the next highest being Two Clubs, and so on, up to the highest possible bid, which is Seven No-trump.

In bidding, a player may *Pass* along to the next bidder. After three passes in a row, the last bid stands. A player may *Double* an opposing bid, meaning the hand will be played a double score, win or lose. An opponent may then *Redouble* that. These are sandwiched between regular bids, and are wiped out if bidding goes higher.

Starting with South, bids might run, S:Pass; W:Pass; N:1S; E:2H; S:Double; W:Redouble; N:3D; E:Pass; S:3S; W:Pass; N:Pass; E:Pass. Bid of Three Spades stands, but North is declarer, as he made the first Spade bid for his team. If South had gone Three No-trump instead of Three Spades, South would become declarer.

The player to declarer's left leads first. Immediately, declarer's partner puts his hand on the table, arranged in suits face up, so declarer can play it as a *dummy* hand. As in Whist, any card may be led, and players must follow suit if possible. Highest of that suit wins, unless a trick is trumped. Winner of trick leads to next. This applies to the dummy hand, so naturally the declarer works neatly back and forth, which is one of the intriguing factors in Bridge. At the end of the hand, tricks are counted and scored; the deal then moves along to the left. If all pass, the hand is dead, and deal simply moves along.

Contract, the type of Bridge played universally today, is so-called because of its special scoring features. Teams seek to win *Rubber*, which is best out of three Games. Once a team has won a game, it becomes *Vulnerable* and receives bonus scores for certain bids; but is also subject to penalties for failing to make *contract.*

A special scoring pad is used, with columns headed *We*

and *They* and a line across the center. Scores for successful bids are marked below the line; and count toward game. All bonus scores go above the line, as per the following schedule.

Each Trick over a Book of Six

	Normal	Doubled	Redoubled
Clubs *or* Diamonds	20	40	80
Hearts *or* Spades	30	60	120
No-trump			
First trick	40	80	160
Added tricks	30	60	120

Game is 100 points. Normally it requires a bid of Five Clubs or Diamonds, Four Hearts or Spades, or Three No-trump, to make Game in a single hand.

Extra tricks are not scored below the line. So a declarer who bids Three Spades and takes five tricks is credited with a *trick score* of 90 below the line, which represents the extent of the bid, and 60 above.

Game is won by the first team making 100 or more points. A line is drawn under the scores and a new game begins. A team is Vulnerable when it has won a Game. This has a bearing on bonus scores and changes the bidding patterns. Best of 2 Games is a Rubber. Scores are then added and a lower total is subtracted from the higher to determine the winner's margin. Scores both below and above the line go in the final total. The latter are bonus points based on the following schedule.

Each Extra Trick over Contract

	Normal	Doubled	Redoubled
Clubs *or* Diamonds	20	100	200
Vulnerable	20	200	400
Hearts *or* Spades	30	100	200
Vulnerable	30	200	400
No-trump	30	100	200
Vulnerable	30	200	400

Making Contract when Doubled *or* Redoubled 50 points

Penalties for Each Trick under Contract

	Normal	Doubled	Redoubled
First Trick	50	100	200
Vulnerable	100	200	400
Every Added Trick	50	200	400
Vulnerable	100	300	600

Scored above the Line in the Opponent's Column.

Other Bonus Scores, Above the Line

	Small Slam	Grand Slam 13 Tricks
Bidding and Making	500	1000
Vulnerable	750	1500

Doubling and Redoubling do not figure into this

Winning Rubber, 2 Games out of 3...........500 points
    Opponents failed to win a game..........200 points
An Unfinished Rubber
    One team only has won a game, the score is......
....300 points
    One team only has part score toward game........
....50 points

Bonus for Honors, Above the Line
All five trump honors—A,K,Q,J,10—in one hand........
....150 points
Four of trump honors in one player's hand....100 points
All four Aces in one hand during No-trump game........
....150 points

Counting and Bidding the Hands. Many modes of counting the hand have been devised, but the simplest is to rate the higher holdings as Ace:4; King:3; Queen:2; Jack:1; Ten:½. Drop 1 point if the hand lacks an Ace, and don't count the Tens unless you have higher cards in the same suit. So the total count of 42 can be regarded as 39.

Divide 39 by 13 and the result is 3. There are thirteen tricks in a Bridge hand, so you can count on 3 points to win a trick. That is your bidding basis, but there are other factors

to be considered. You may be short on points, but if you are
long on trumps and other suits, they will take tricks, too. So
you can count extra cards in any suit as the equivalent of
high card points.

It works like this. The perfectly balanced hand of thirteen
cards contains different suits in the proportion: 4 3 3 3. If
you have 10 points, consisting of, A, K, Q, J in different
suits, this represents an average hand. The suit with four
cards should be your trump suit.

Now, if the hand is unbalanced, the longest suit should
preferably be the trump, so each card beyond four is worth 1
point. Similarly, each card beyond three in any other suit is
worth 1 point. This enables you to evaluate a hand as follows:

♠: A,J,8,3   ♦: Q,5,4   ♣: K,6,2   ♥: 10,9,7

There are 10 points for high cards: A, K, Q, J with a possible ½ for the 10. But if the hand should be:

♠: A,J,9,8,7   ♦: Q,5,4,3   ♣: K,10,6,2

There would still be 10, or 10½, points for high cards, but
there is also 1 point for a fifth trump, Spades, and 1 each for
fourth cards in other suits, Diamonds and Clubs, giving the
hand 13½ points. With 12 points good for 4 tricks, at 3
points each, you are working on a potential fifth point, justi-
fying a bid of One Spade.

Here, you expect your partner to deliver two tricks, a normal prospect. The more points you have, the less such help
you need. If your hand has 21 points, it is the equivalent of 7
tricks and needs no help. So that is the limit of the normal
One bid.

With 22 points you are working on your eighth trick, with
no help needed, so you can bid Two if you hold a majority,
seven, of the trump, so the opposition cannot out trump you.

With 23 or 24, six trumps should suffice. With 25 points, you have the equivalent of 8 tricks, at 3 points each, and are working on a ninth, so a bid of Two is about certain with five trump in hand.

However, you need strong trump, with high cards, and a strong second suit is also helpful in bidding Two. If in doubt, bid One in order to sound out your partner, because Two is regarded as *forcing* your partner to make a bid toward game, no matter how poor his hand may be. So the higher the point count, the better the Two bid.

An opening bid of Three or more is generally used to *shut out* your opponents from bidding and at the same time warn your partner that you have a low value in points with a long trump suit. As an example, this hand with eight Diamonds, headed by the Q,J.

♠: Q,8   ♥: 6,5   ♦: Q,J,9,8,7,6,4,2   ♣: 9

There would be 2 points for the Queen, 1 for the Jack and 4 for the added trumps, a total of only 7. With 2 more for an odd counter like the Q♠, it still would have only 9 points. But the hand can take six tricks with trumps and any help from your partner might make a Three bid good. If you go down, it may be worth it, since you have blocked your adversaries from any intelligent bidding.

Some bidders go Three on a 7-card suit and Four on an 8-card suit. But once the point count reaches 13, a One bid is the accepted rule.

No-trump bids require a hand of 4 3 3 3 suit pattern or at least a hand with only one *Doubleton*, two-card suit, as 4 4 3 2 or 5 3 3 2. Count high cards only, excluding ½ point for a Ten and make sure of *stoppers* in three suits and a stopper or partial stopper in the fourth. Bid One No-trump on a count of 16, 17 or 18. *Examples:*

♠: A,J,5	♥: Q,10,7	♦: A,9,5,4	♣: K,Q,3	16 points
♠: A,K	♥: A,Q,7,5	♦: K,9,7,2	♣: J,9,4	17 points
♠: K,J	♥: A,J,9	♦: Q,J,7,5,4	♣: A,Q,9	18 points

A count of 16, 17 or 18 representing as many as six tricks, at 3 points each, is indicative of No-trump strength and therefore worth the One bid. With 19, 20 or 21, six tricks are *in* and you are working on a seventh. It's too good for a One bid and not strong enough for Two. Here, a bid of One Club indicates that you may have such an in-between hand, but if one suit is particularly strong it is often wise to bid it. The One Club bid is a universally accepted bid that indicates strength, but without length in a strong suit.

A count of 22, 23 or 24 puts you in the Two bid bracket, but you must have a sure stopper in every suit; no mere partials. *As examples:*

♠: A,Q,7	♥: A,9,8,2	♦: A,Q,5,3	♣: Q,J	22 points
♠: A,Q	♥: A,K,9	♦: J,9,8,7,5	♣: A,K,Q	23 points
♠: A,J	♥: Q,J,9	♦: A,K,J,6	♣: A,K,J,8	24 points

If you are lucky enough to have a reasonably balanced hand, 4 3 3 3, 4 4 3 2, 5 3 3 2, with 25, 26, or 27 points, with stoppers in all suits, you can bid Three No-trump, as with the following.

♠: A,K,Q	♥: A,J	♦: K,Q,6,3,2	♣: K,Q,J	25 points
♠: A,Q,7	♥: A,9,8,5	♦: A,K	♣: A,K,J,8	26 points
				note: 5 for 4th Ace
♠: A,Q,J	♥: A,K,5	♦: K,Q,J,2	♣: A,K	27 points

In response to a bid, your partner rates his hand and with less than 6 points, he should Pass, admitting his hand is that weak. If he has four of your trumps and a 6 to 10 count, he can raise your bid to Two. With three trumps that have a count of 1½ or more, he can raise on 7 to 10. With such hands, he can add 1 point for a *Singleton*, lone card, in an odd suit, and 2 points for a *void*, no cards in an odd suit.

With your 13 and his 6, the total of 19 indicates six tricks, at 3 points each, with a potential seventh, but a trump *fit* makes it worth Two. Remember that this is a minimum; with

14 and 7, there would be a sure 21, while often the opening bid is based on higher pointage.

If your partner has a total of 13 points and support in your suit, he should raise your suit bid to Three. You must then bid on up to Game between you, as two *opening hands* in tandem have more than a 9-trick potential indicated by 26 or 27. They can take ten or eleven tricks and maybe more. This is called a *jump bid*.

If your partner has a regular count of 6 to 10 points but lacks trump support, he can respond with a One bid in his suit. That's impossible if you opened with One Heart—his suit being Clubs or Diamonds. In those cases he can bid One No-trump if he has 6 to 10 points in high cards alone.

In any case, One over One, as such a bid is known, forces you to make another bid unless an opponent intervenes. If your partner has 11 to 18 points with a biddable suit, but lacks support in your suit, he should raise to One in a higher ranking suit (if that is his biddable suit), or to Two, in a lower ranking suit.

If you opened with One Spade, he could go Two Diamonds.

Whatever his new suit, you can regard it as an opening bid on his part, and count up your hand to see if you can support it with a Two or even a Three bid if necessary. If your own trump is strong and long, you can rebid it at Two. Otherwise, you may bid a new suit if it has an opening count, or bid One or even Two No-trump, depending on your partner's suit for help.

If you open with One No-trump, your partner may Pass with less than 8 points, or bid Two in a long suit. With 10 points and up, he can go Three in strong suit, or bid Three No-trump if he has a balanced hand. If he can help your No-trump with a balanced hand of his own, he should do so.

Here, he can use the yardstick of "3 points to a trick," applying it to the high cards only. He figures your One No-trump as 16 minimum, so he needs about 8 to make it 24 with an exact bid of Two No-trump. He needs about 11 to make it 27 for a Three bid, and so on. If you open with Two No-trump, signifying 22, he should aim for the same totals; but the bidding must be continued until Game is reached.

Going for *Slam* is an exciting phase of Bridge, and expert players use artificial *asking bids* to learn how many Aces or Kings a partner holds. The data is furnished by coded responses, known however to both teams. These so-called *conventions* vary, and must be mutually acceptable by opposing teams, hence they go beyond the range of basic Bridge.

Defensive Bidding is used to counteract the opening bids of the opposition. The simplest form is the Overcall where you bid like a responder, but against the opening bidder, not with him.

To overcall with One, as One Spade over an opponent's One Heart, you need 10 points, with connecting honors in a five-card or preferably six-card trump, as:

| ♠: K,Q,J,9,7 | ♥: 9,6 | ♦: 9,8,2 | ♣: K,10,9 |
| ♠: Q,J,10,9,7,6 | ♥: 8,3,2 | ♦: A,7,3 | ♣: 5 |

To overcall with Two over One, as Two Diamonds over One Heart, you need 12 points with strong trump honors and a six-card trump.

| ♠: A,8,6 | ♥: 7,2 | ♦: K,Q,J,9,8,6 | ♣: 5,4 |
| ♥: K,10,9 | ♥: 3 | ♦: A,K,9,8,6,2 | ♣: 6,4,2 |

Tricks may take precedence over points in many overcalls. With a strong 7-card suit or a hand approaching 16 points, you can jump an overcall, as Three Diamonds over One Spade. This has a shutout effect and tips your partner to your hand. A most effective overcall is One No-trump over an opposing One in a suit. All you need is a normal One No-trump holding, provided it includes stoppers in the suit the opponent bid.

The *takeout Double* is another defensive bid. You use it

when you are short on the suit bid by an opponent, but have good holdings in the other three. You treat it as an opening bid, with the 13-point requirement, but in an unnamed suit, as you leave that to your partner. As an ideal example:

♠: 3   ♥: A,10,9,2   ♦: K,J,8,7   ♣: Q,J,9,3

Opponent bids One Spade. You Double which forces your partner to bid his preferred suit. Your high cards add up to 11½, but whatever trump he names—♥, ♦, ♣—you have the required support of four cards, with an extra card, one more than three, in two other suits. You also have a Singleton Spade, so the 3 added points give you 14½ which exceeds the required 13.

As another hand:

♠: 8,5   ♥: K,Q,3   ♦: A,J,7,3   ♣: Q,J,9

Opponent bids One Spade and you Double. Your high cards total 13. If your partner bids Hearts or Clubs, you are one card short in trump support, but make it up with the extra in the odd suit, Diamonds, so your 13 stands. If he bids Diamonds your count becomes 14.

To distinguish a *takeout* from a *business* Double, keep these facts in mind. You can't make a takeout Double if your partner has done anything but Pass. You must make the takeout Double the first time you have a chance to double a bid of that suit. A Double of a bid of Four or more is a business Double.

Any double of a No-trump bid is a business Double, although your partner may take you out if you Double One No-trump. Occasionally, with a freakish hand, a partner may take you out of another business Double, but rarely.

If you make a takeout Double and the next player bids higher or redoubles, your partner does not have to take you out, but can let the bidding come around to you. Otherwise, your partner's takeout is similar to a response of an opening bid in the suit he most prefers; so often, he can follow that accepted bidding pattern. If you have Doubled an opposing bid of Two or Three, your partner still must take you out. Afterward, you can consider your rebid, if any.

CANASTA

A South American game resembling a glorified form of
Rummy, played with two or more packs. It has almost as
many *wild* variants as Poker, some of which have been stan-
dardized under special names, as will be mentioned. All stem
from the basic game, which has four players forming two
pair of partners seated opposite, A. and C vs. B and D. A
double pack is used, with two Jokers from each pack, making
108 cards in all.

Eleven cards are dealt to each player and the pack is
placed face down in the center of the table, with one card
being turned face up beside it, to begin a discard pile known
as *El Pozo* or The Pot. A special tray with two compartments
is often used to receive the pack and discards.

Play starts with A, who is to the left of the dealer, D. It
continues around the circle. Each player draws a card from
the pack; he then may make a meld, by laying down certain
combinations of cards if he has them and wants to meld

29

them; finally, he discards a single card from his hand, placing
it face up on the pot.

Under certain conditions, a player may draw from the pot
instead of the pack, but in so doing, he must take up the entire pot. This is the great aim in Canasta, as the more cards a
player holds, the bigger his melding opportunities, all with
scoring values. The basic values of the cards are as follows:

Each Joker, four wild cards	*50 points*
Each Deuce, eight wild cards	*20 points*
Each Ace, eight natural cards	*20 points*
Each King, Queen, Jack, Ten, Nine, Eight, 48 natural cards	*10 points*
Each Seven, Six, Five, Four, 32 natural cards	*5 points*
Each Black Three, 4 stoppers	*5 points*
Each Red Three, 4 bonus cards	*Special*

All melds consist of three or more cards of the same natural rank as K, K, K; 8,8,8,8; etc.; but wild cards can be included, provided the meld contains at least two naturals and
not more than three wild cards.

Allowable	*Not Allowable*
Q, Q, Joker	Q, 2, 2
9, 9, 2, 2	9, 2, 2, 2
7, 7, 7, 7, 2, 2, 2,	7, 7, 7, 2, 2, 2, 2

Cards may be added to a player's meld—or his partner's as
the game progresses, and all are scored according to their individual values. Thus K, K, K would be 30; while Q, Q,
Joker would be 70; and 9, 9, 2, 2 would be 60.

However, when a group of seven or more cards is melded
it is called *Canasta* or *Basket*, and adds a bonus to the score.
The bonus is 500 points for a *Natural Canasta*, with all cards
alike, as K, K, K, K, K, K, K or 6, 6, 6, 6, 6, 6, 6, 6, but
only 300 points for a *Mixed Canasta*, which includes one or
more wild cards, as 10, 10, 10, 10, 2, 2, 2 or J, J, J, J, J, J, J, J,
2.

After melding a 7-card Canasta, an eighth card may be added, but a player must avoid adding a wild card to a Natural Canasta, as its 500 bonus would drop to 300 for a Mixed Canasta. A meld of J, J, J, J, J, J, J is worth 570 as it stands, and adding the last Jack would make it 580. But adding a Joker instead, would cut it to 420. But a player who has melded a 7-card Mixed Canasta, say: J, J, J, J, 2, 2, 2, has only 300 bonus points anyway, with a total of 400, so adding another wild card like a Joker would up it to 450.

Note that in this case, the 8-card Canasta would have four wild cards with its J, J, J, J, 2, 2, 2, Joker. Ordinarily, only three wild cards are allowable in a meld, but a fourth can be tacked on after a 7-card Canasta has been melded.

Two questions come up early in Canasta play. Are sequences as: 6, 7, 8 allowable as melds? Can wild cards be melded in a group as: 2, 2, 2? The answer is an emphatic NO to both questions, according to the standard game of Canasta. But such melds can figure in some of the variants to be described later.

Tres Colorados, or the Red Threes, should be mentioned here. They are special cards, with bonus values, that do not figure in the melding or the regular play. If a player is dealt a Red Three, he should declare it on his first turn, by placing it face up on the table and drawing another card from the pack to replace it. If later he draws a Red Three, he should then declare it and draw another card.

Each Red Three counts 100 points for the player who declares it, so it is kept with his meld. If a team declares all four Red Threes, their value is doubled from 400 to 800. However, if a team is unable to meld, it loses those points at the end of the hand.

It is important to meld a Canasta, not only to get the bonus points, but because a team must make such a meld before one of its members melds all his cards and ends the hand by going out. His team gets 100 points for going out, and if he goes out by laying down his hand all at once—with

no previous melds—he gets another 100 points. However, he
must lay down a complete Canasta, if he goes out *concealed*,
as this is termed; he is not allowed, in this case, to lay off on
his partner's hand.

In order to take up the pot, one member of a team must
make an initial meld of 50 points or more. This can be done
in more than one meld, but combined, they must meet the 50
point minimum, by one player. Until then, the pot is frozen
against the team.

This means that the pot can only be taken by matching its
uppermost card with two, or more, of the same value; that is,
by a *natural* meld. With a Queen as upcard, this would demand showing two Queens from the hand; not a Queen and
Deuce. It is allowable to use the upcard as part of an opening
meld, provided that an additional meld brings the total to the
necessary 50.

As an illustration, suppose a Queen is upcard. A player has
two Queens, two Sixes and a Deuce. With the upcard, he
melds: Q, Q, Q, 2, 6, 6. These total 30 each, making more
than 50. Melding the wild Deuce with the Sixes is all right, as
it is a separate meld and does not involve the upcard.

As the game progresses, higher opening melds are de-
manded. When a team drops under zero, it needs only 15
points to open; from 0 to 1495 it needs 50 points; from 1500
to 2995 it needs 90 points and over 3000 the team requires
120 points to open.

The pot is also frozen if a Red Three is dealt as the original upcard, and a player can freeze it at any time by simply
discarding a wild card, Deuce or Joker. Regardless of
whether a team has made its opening minimum, the pot is
frozen against both sides if any of those cards are in it.
Again, a meld of three natural cards as: 9, 9, 9 is necessary
to take the pot.

When the pot is no longer frozen, it can be taken with any
meld of three cards as: 2, 8, 8, or simply adding the upcard
to an existing meld belonging to the team. Suppose an Eight

is the upcard. A player can take it, and the pot with it, if he or his partner has already made a meld of three Eights, 8, 8, 8 or 2, 8, 8, he uses the upcard as the fourth Eight and takes all the other cards from the pot into his own hand.

Black Threes cannot be melded until a player goes out, when he may meld them like other cards. If a player discards a Black Three, it has the effect of freezing the pot against the next player, as he cannot match a Black Three in ordinary fashion. But as soon as another card is discarded, the Black Three has no effect, as it is buried. But the pack stays frozen when any wild card is in it.

Discarding a wild card or a Black Three is part of a team's strategy when it wishes to make it harder for the other side to take the pot.

After a player has melded a Canasta he may *go out* whenever he wishes, provided he is able to meld all his cards or all but the one which he discards. He may ask his partner for permission to go out, and then go by what his partner says for that turn; but this is optional.

When a player goes out, each team adds all its points for Red Threes, Canastas, for going out, by the team that does so, and for all melded cards, according to their specified point values. Players then show any cards left in their hands and those points are deducted from the team score.

Where points are concerned, a player has just two advantages in going out. His team gets a bonus of 100 points, or 200 if he goes out concealed; and his own hand is immune from deductions, though his partner's is not. Thus there are times when the team that goes out is outscored by its opponents.

Game is 5000 points. If one or both teams goes over that, the team with the higher score wins the difference in points. These are counted at the end of the final hand, which is played through.

Penalties are applied in Canasta in the following ways.

Red Threes count against a player if still in his hand when

someone goes out. Values of Red Threes vary in some games. Black Threes may also be given special penalty losses.

Drawing out of turn or taking the pot illegally carries 100 points' penalty, but this is not invoked unless the player loses the drawn card in his hand, or mixes the pot so it is hard to identify the cards and replace them.

If a player makes an incorrect opening meld, his team is forced to add 10 points to open. If he takes back cards after melding, it costs him 100 points. Any mistake in *going out* costs 100 points.

There are many variations of Canasta, some of which have become games in themselves. All may be *stepped up* by special rules, so they are given here in brief.

Canasta with Two Players

The usual game, but with only two persons, each getting 15 cards in the deal. Player can meld only on his own, and two Canastas are needed to go out.

Canasta with Three Players

Regular Canasta but with each player getting 13 cards in the deal, and each playing on his own, with only one Canasta needed to go out. This game can be varied, by having two players combine as partners against the first one who takes the pot in any hand.

Canasta with Six Players

Played either by three teams of two players each, with opposite players as partners; or by two teams of three each, composed of alternating players. Each is dealt 11 cards; but sometimes three packs are used, with 13 cards dealt to each player.

Canasta With Wild Melds

Regular Canasta, but a player may meld wild cards, Jokers and Deuces, by themselves. These count at face value, and a *Wild Canasta* of seven cards counts 2000 points and is the limit of such a meld. The pack is always frozen in this game which is called *Uruguay* or *Uruguayan Canasta,* though the latter title also refers to an earlier form of Canasta.

Players may be dealt 13 cards in the four-handed *wild meld* game, and the goal may be set at 7500 points. This definitely applies in a form called *Cuban Canasta* in which *extra wild* Canastas figure. Any wild meld is 2000; a wild with four Jokers, 3000; a wild with no Jokers, 4000. When game is 7500, an opening meld of 150 is required at the 5000 mark. Each additional Red Three gives a player an extra 100 points in this game, with all four counting 1000.

Three-Pack Canasta

Three-Pack Canasta can be played with less than six players, either in simple form, or with wild melds allowable. It includes types called *Chilean Canasta* and *Mexican Canasta,* but these have largely given way to Samba, which has special features of its own, as well as other games, all with three packs.

Samba

Basically like Canasta, Samba requires three packs, with two Jokers each, making 162 cards in all. Its great feature is that players may meld a sequence of three or more cards in one suit, seven such cards ♥: J, 10, 9, 8, 7, 6, 5 become a special Canasta known as a Samba. No wild cards are allowed in a Samba. Cards may run from Ace, high, down to Four, low, but seven is the limit.

A Samba counts 1500 points. A Natural Canasta counts the usual 500 points and may contain seven or eight cards of the same value. A Mixed Canasta is 300 points, but can contain only two wild cards, not three, among the first seven cards. A Samba or a Canasta can be started with three cards and built further as in the game of Canasta.

In the four-player game, each is dealt 15 cards, not just 11. Each player draws two cards from the pack, but discards only one, so his hand increases whether he takes the pot or not. To take the pot, one player on a team must show a minimum meld, but these run: below zero: 15; zero to 1495: 50; 1500 to 1995: 90; 3000 to 6995: 120; 7000 and over: 150. Game is 10,000.

As in Canasta, the pot is frozen to start, so a player must match the upcard with two *naturals* to take the pot. After that it still requires two naturals, but a player can also take the pot by adding the upcard to a meld already made, either in value or sequence. If he has melded 10, 10, 10 a player may add any 10 that happens to be an upcard; if he has melded ♥: J, 10, 9 he may add either the Q♥ or 8♥ if one is an upcard.

But he cannot add an upcard to a completed 7-card Canasta or Samba. Nor can he match an upcard with a wild and natural card, like combining a Joker and Six from the hand with a Six as upcard. Nor can he use the upcard to start a sequence as ♦: 8, 7, 6.

To go out, a team must first meld two Canastas, a Samba rating as a sequence Canasta. When a player goes out, his team scores 200 points, with nothing extra for going out concealed. Red Threes are worth 100 each as in Canasta, with all six scoring 1000. However, unless a team melds two Canastas, Red Threes count against it and are deducted.

In a stepped up form of Samba called *Bolivia,* players may meld wild cards, beginning with three and going up to a wild card Canasta of seven which is a Bolivia and counts 2500. A Samba counts 1500 as usual, and regular Canastas 500 if natural and if with wild cards 300. Game is usually set at 15,000.

Other variations of Samba allow one wild card in a Samba, or sequence Canasta, and make the opening meld a Canasta when at the 8000 level. Sometimes a rule is made that the pot is always frozen. With six players four packs may be used with game set at 20,000 points. National titles, as Brazilian and Italian Canasta are given to such games, but so many rules are arbitrary or interchangeable that the simplest way is to enumerate them in detail beforehand.

In wild games, Black Threes are often counted as 100 each against players caught with them, though they are only worth 5 points each to the player who melds them when going out. Another and highly popular rule is to regard Black Threes exactly like Red Threes, but as a separate item, being scored at the same values.

CASINO

A good game for two players, or for four, paired as partners. Can also be played by three, opposing one another. It consists of matching or taking cards that are face up on the table; and at the finish of each hand, the players compare their *take* and score as follows:

Most cards	*3 points*
Most Spades	*1 point*
Big Casino: 10♦	*2 points*
Little Casino: 2♠	*1 point*
Each Ace	*1 point*

In addition, one point is given to a player each time he *sweeps* the board of all cards showing there. In skilled play, sweeps are sometimes disallowed by agreement.

The deal consists of four cards dealt face down and singly to each player, plus four cards dealt face up in the center of the table. The pack is retained face down by the dealer, for further dealing.

The player at the dealer's left may then do any of the following.

He may *take* one of the face up cards by matching it with a card of the same value from his hand, as a six with a six, or a Queen with a Queen.

He may *combine* two or more cards on the table and take them with a card of that value, as 2 and 5 equal 7, taken with a Seven; Ace, 3 and 6 equal 10, taken with a Ten. Aces count as one in combinations; Jacks, Queens, Kings, have no numerical value; in addition, suits have no importance.

He may also *build* by adding a card from his hand to one on the board and naming their total, as the 3♥ on the 5♠, which would be called *Eight*. But he must have a card of the higher value in his hand, as the 8♦, to take the build on his next play; otherwise, the build is illegal.

Two combinations can be taken at once; if the board showed A♣, 6♥, 5♣, 2♥ the player could put the A♣ on the 6♥ and the 2♥ on the 5♣ then take them both with the 7♦ from his hand.

Similarly, a build can be doubled. If the player had the 2♠ and 8♦ in his hand, he could put the 5♣, 2♥, A♣ in a pile saying Eight; then add the 2♠ from his hand to the 6♥, saying Eight, then put both groups together, calling the build Eights and take the whole with the 8♦ on his next turn.

If unable to match, combine or build, a player must discard, placing a card from his hand with the face up row, of which it becomes a part. Often a player discards a court card J, Q, or K as it offers an opponent no help in combinations or builds.

There are two hazards in a build. First, an opponent may build it higher. Thus, if Player A puts the 3♦ from his hand on the 4♠ on the table and says Seven, intending to take it with the 7♣ later, Player B, holding the A♣ and the 8♠, could add the Ace to the build and say Eight.

The only way to prevent this is by the *double* build already described, as another player cannot add to such a build. That is a good reason for making it whenever possible.

The other hazard is simply that the opposing player may take the build as it stands. If A puts the 3♦ on the 4♠ and says Seven, B can gobble it up with the 7♠ if he is holding that card. That is the risk that Player A must take.

A build always stands as stated. Thus, a player can put the 3♠ on the 3♦ and call it Threes as a double build, or he could add 3 and 3 to equal 6 and call it Six. But if A says, Three, B cannot take it with a six, or vice versa.

Also, in increasing a build, a player must add a card from his own hand. If A puts the 3♦ on the 4♠ and says Seven, B cannot pick up a Deuce that is showing on the board and add it to the build to form Nine. He would have to hold a Deuce and a Nine of his own, adding the Deuce from his hand and hoping to take the increased build with the Nine on his next play.

Once a player has made a build, he must take it on his next turn, unless he can take some other card or combination, or make another build. He cannot throw a discard while his own build is waiting for him to take it.

Good players are always alert for sweeps. In a two-handed game, a player might see three cards as 4♠, 2♦, 3♦ on the board and clear it by taking them with the 9♥. He then turns one of the cards face up in his pile, to indicate 1 point for a sweep. If his opponent should then discard a Jack and he happened to have a Jack himself, he could take it for another sweep.

After each player has used the four cards dealt him, the dealer deals another round of four to each and the game continues. This is done in succeeding rounds until the pack is used up. At the finish, any cards on the board go to the player who took the last trick, but that does not count as a sweep.

There are two ways of scoring in Casino. One is to call each hand a game and settle accordingly. The other is to play until one player reaches 21, which makes him the winner. In approaching 21, a player may call out if he thinks he has enough points. If he is correct he wins; otherwise, he loses.

Let us assume that Player A has 19 points and Player B has 16. In the course of the next deal, Player A knows that B could take the majority of points, say 8, and win the game. Thus aware, as soon as A has gathered in two points, which gives him a total of 21, he calls out that he has the required number of points to win.

If nobody calls out, whoever has the highest total wins. However, in case of a tie, it may be mutually agreed to continue on another 11 points, which can be repeated until one player's win is undisputed.

In three-handed Casino, ties in cards count 3 points, Spades count 1 point, are fairly frequent. In case of such ties, in any type of game, nobody scores the points in question. In four-handed Casino, the partners, seated opposite, combine their scores as a team. In standard Casino, face cards cannot be used to build. A Jack can take only another Jack, even if there are two on the board. Otherwise, it would eliminate the chance for sweeps in many games. However, face cards can be used to build in Royal Casino.

Royal Casino

In this case, each Jack is regarded as 11; each Queen: 12; each King: 13. Builds are higher proportionately, making it possible to *overbuild* three or four times. For those who like it, Aces may be rated as either 1 or 14. In games where that is allowed, players may also agree that once a build of 14 has been announced as Ace, the build can be regarded as 1 and be continued up from there. Furthermore, there is a variety of Royal Casino where the Two of Spades is either a 2 or 15, and the Ten of Diamonds is either 10 or 16.

Scoring is the same as in regular Casino.

Spade Casino

This has a different scoring table than the standard game. There are 24 points in each hand, namely:

Cards: 3, Big Casino: 2, Little Casino: 2, Jack of Spades: 2, Ace of Spades: 2, other Aces: 1 each, all other Spades: 1 each.

The game can be played on a Regular or Royal basis.

Draw Casino

This differs from standard Casino purely in procedure. After each play, a player draws the top card from the pack to replenish his hand and bring it up to its original 4-card quota. This continues, eliminating the customary redeals of four cards used in the regular game. Hands are played through to the last card, as usual.

Any type of Casino, Regular, Royal, Spade or Spade-Royal, can be played in "draw" fashion.

CRIBBAGE

One of the most popular of two-handed games, Cribbage, is played with a 52-card pack, with the face cards valued at 10 each, and the rest according to their figures: 10, 9 and so on down to Ace for 1. As sequences form part of the scoring, cards rank from King down to Ace: K, Q, J, 10, 9, 8, 7, 6, 5, 4, 3, 2, A.

As a two-handed game, Cribbage can be described in terms of Players A and B, with the latter as the dealer. B deals cards singly, face down, to A and himself, six cards to each. They look at their hands and each lays two cards face down. These discards are placed together, and become the *Crib*.

Now A cuts the pack and B turns up the top card of the lower half, placing it on the upper. This card is called the *Starter* and serves a special function later. For the moment, if it happens to be a Jack, it is honored with the title of *His Heels* and the dealer scores 2 points announcing, "Two for His Heels."

Score may be kept with paper and pencil, but it is better

with a cribbage board, which has a series of holes in regular order, and pegs for each player. So in scoring *Two for His Heels* the dealer immediately pegs two holes.

Player A now puts a card from his hand face up on the table in front of him, and calls its value, such as Four, for the 4♠. Player B, the dealer, does the same with a card from his hand, adding its value to A's and stating the total, thus, if B should play the 3♥, he would say Seven.

As this continues, a player may add a card which enables him to peg points.

Pair of same rank in succession	*2 points*
Three of a Kind in succession	*6 points*
Four of a Kind in succession	*12 points*
Three or more cards, a sequence, *each card*	*1 point*
Fifteen as a total	*2 points*
Total of Thirty-One	*2 points*

As an illustration, suppose A and B played alternately:

A	6♣	3♥	4♦
B	6♦	5♣	7♦

B would peg two for a Pair 6 and 6. A would peg two for Fifteen 6, 6 and 3. B would not peg on his next play, but A would peg four for a sequence of four cards 6, 3, 5 and 4. On the next play, B would peg five for a sequence of five cards 6, 3, 5, 4 and 7.

In addition, B would score two points for attaining a total of Thirty-one. Cards are then turned down in front of each player and the other player, in this case A, begins a new count by playing another card.

It is not always possible to hit an exact count of Thirty-one, and a player is not allowed to go beyond that total. If he falls short, he declares, *Go,* and the other player proceeds to put down whatever cards he can without going over 31. If he is unable to hit 31, he scores one point for continuing on Go. If he is unable to Go, the first player scores the point.

As an illustration, suppose A and B played alternately:

A	K♦	4♣
B	Q♥	2♦

The count has now reached 26, and assuming that A has only the 6♣ and the 10♦, he cannot play either without going over 31, so he says Go. B, who has the 3♣ and the 5♦, plays the 3♣, pegging three points for that many cards in sequence 4, 2, 3; and he also scores one point for being able to Go. But he can go no further, so cards are turned down.

It is then A's turn, so he plays the 6♣, saying Six. B plays the 5♦, saying Eleven. A plays the 10♦, saying Twenty-one. Both are out of cards, so A scores another special point for Last Card, which is practically the same as a Go that B is unable to follow up.

If one players runs out of cards, the other continues to play alone, scoring and pegging on his own, just as if his adversary still happened to be in the hand, until all cards have been played.

Notes on scoring during the play.

With picture cards, Pairs must be of the same rank, as: K and K, Q and Q, J and J. A Pair cannot be formed by K and Q or K and J, even though the cards themselves are valued at 10 points each in the count. The same applies to Three or Four of a Kind.

Sequences do not have to be in actual order, as long as there are no gaps between. The following 7, 4, 6 is not a sequence, due to the gap. Add a Five, making 7, 4, 6, 5 and it is a four-card sequence. Add a Two—7, 4, 6, 5, 2—and it does not count. But add a Three to that setup, forming 7, 4, 6, 5, 2, 3 and it becomes a six-card sequence, good for six points.

After the hands have been played and turned down, more pegging follows, by scoring combinations within each hand itself. Player A begins by turning his hand face up, and counting combinations, enumerated in the chart following, including the Starter as a wild card, thus giving his hand the equivalent of five cards, not just four. He counts the combinations aloud as he pegs them.

Player B, the dealer, then does the same with his hand, also including the Starter as a wild card. That done, B turns up the discarded crib and as dealer, he has the privilege of counting and pegging its points for himself, again with the starter as a wild card.

The scoring combinations are as follows.

Each Pair of same rank	2 *points*
Each card in sequence of three or more	1 *point*
Each Fifteen formed	2 *points*
Flush: All cards of starter suit	5 *points*
Flush: Four cards of another suit	4 *points*
Counts in hand; but not in crib	
His Nobs, Jack of starter suit	1 *point*

Three of a Kind, originally known as a Pair Royal, still count 6 because they add up as separate Pairs. Thus K♦, K♣, K♥ actually consist of three Pairs: K♦ and K♥, K♦ and K♥, K♣ and K♥, which at two points each, make six. Similarly, Four of a Kind, or Double Pair Royal, counts 12. A hand like 9♥, 9♣, 9♠, 9♦ makes six Pairs: 9♥ and 9♣; 9♥ and 9♠, 9♥ and 9♦; 9♣ and 9♠; 9♣ and 9♦; 9♠ and 9♦.

Sequences allow for double or multiple count, provided there is a duplicate of one or more cards. A sequence of three cards with one duplicate would count 8 points, thus K♥, Q♦, J♥, Q♠. The count would be 3 for sequence K♥, Q♦, J♥; 3 for sequence K♥, Q♠, J♥; 2 for Pair; Q♦ and Q♠.

Fifteens, at 2 points each, can be multiplied as with this hand: 9♦, 6♣, 5♥, 4♠, 2♦. Here, 15 can be counted three ways 9♦, 6♣; 9♦, 4♥, 2♦; 6♣, 5♥, 4♠ for six points; plus 3 points for the sequence 6♣, 5♥, 4♠; or a total of points.

Here are samples of much bigger combinations running from the highest possible down:

Four Fives, one a starter, and a Jack of starter suit	29

This adds up: Four of a Kind, 12; four Fifteens formed by Fives, 8; four Fifteens, Jack with each Five, 8; His Nobs, 1.

Four Fives with a Ten or face card	28
Two Fives, two Fours and a Six, *or* two Fives, two Sixes and a Four, *or* two Fours, two Sixes and a Five, *or* two Sevens, two Eights, and a Nine	24

These add up to four Fifteens, 8; four sequences of three cards, 12; two Pairs, 4.

Four Threes and a Nine	24

Four of a Kind, 12; six Fifteens, 12.

Three Fives, a Four and a Six	23
Three Fours, a Five and a Six, *or* three Sixes, a Four and a Five, *or* three Sevens, an Eight and Nine, *or* three Eights, a Seven and Nine	21

Three Fifteens for 6; Three of a Kind, 6; three sequences of three cards, 9.

Four Deuces and a Nine; *or* four Threes and a Six	20
Two Sixes, two Sevens and an Eight, *or* two Sevens, an Eight and Nine, *or* two Eights, a Seven and two Nines	20
*Three Tens, or Jacks, Queens, Kings, and two Fives	20
Three Threes and two Nines, *or* three Sevens, two Aces	20

* Any King, Queen, Jack or Ten is known as a tenth card. Mix three tenth cards with a Pair of Fives, as K, J, 10, 5, 5 and the six Fifteens result, counting 12 points; with a Pair of Fives, for a total of 14. Pair two of the tenth cards, as K, J, J, 5, 5 and the count is 16. Put them in sequence K, Q, J, 5, 5 and the count is 17. Make them Three of a Kind and the count is 20 J, J, J, 5, 5. Add 1 point whenever a Jack is His Nobs.

Three Threes and two Sixes	18

Three Threes make 6; Pair of Sixes, 2; each Six combines with the three Threes for a Fifteen, making 4; each Three combines with the two Sixes for a Fifteen, making 6.

Three Fours a Three and a Five	17

Three cards in sequence, two with duplicates, but no Fifteens, as 10♥, 9♣, 8♠, 10♣, 8♥

16

There are four ways to form 10, 9, 8, which make 12, plus two pair for 4.

In counting Fifteens, a player refers to them as Fifteen-two, meaning one Fifteen for two points; Fifteen-four, which is two Fifteens for four points; and so on.

After the hands and crib are counted, the deal changes, so in this case A would deal new hands. In scoring, each player uses two pegs, jumping one ahead of the other, starting at the same end of the board, going up the outside row and down the inside. Twice around and 1 point more wins the game with 121 points.

Scoring 121 before the loser gets to 61 means that the loser is lurched and the winner gets credit for two games. Game can be for 61 points, with 31 needed to avoid being lurched.

Three-Handed Cribbage

In Three-Handed Cribbage, each player is dealt five cards and places one in the crib, so each has four cards, and the crib three, but it is dealt an extra card to make four. Scoring is as usual, and the deal keeps moving to the left.

Five Card Cribbage

Five Card Cribbage is an old form of the game in which two players are dealt five cards each and give two apiece to the crib. Play ends at 31 or Go. Otherwise, it is much like the six card game which has superseded it as the standard form of Cribbage.

ÉCARTÉ

This is a famous French game, a predecessor of Euchre. It is played by two persons with a 32-card pack in which the cards of each suit are valued in the following order: K, Q, J, A, 10, 9, 8, 7.

Five cards are dealt to each person and the next is turned up and laid aside as trump. If it is the King, the dealer credits himself with one point. The first player, or non-dealer, either decides to *accept* the hand, which means that he will play it as it stands; or he can *propose* that the dealer make such a choice.

If either accepts his hand, a player holding the King of trump may show it and mark it as one point on his score. The first player then leads and the dealer must follow suit, going higher if he can. If unable to follow suit, he must trump if possible; otherwise, he can throw away a card from an odd suit.

The player taking a trick leads to the next and the process is repeated. If the one who accepted the hand takes 3 or 4 tricks, he scores one point: for taking all the tricks, called *vole,* he scores two points. Game is five points.

In case neither accepts his hand as is, the first player discards 1 to 5 cards in a face down pile and draws cards from the pack to replace them. The dealer does not have to draw, but can do so if he wishes. Again, each player may accept his hand as it now stands; if so, play proceeds exactly as already described, beginning with the *marking* of the King and a lead by the first player.

Scoring, however, is now on an equal basis. Whichever player wins 3 or 4 tricks is credited with one point; if either player takes all 5 tricks, he gets two points for *la vole.*

If both players reject their hands after the draw, they can discard again on the same basis and try accepting trump, which remains as represented by the turned up card; this cannot be touched. Rejecting and discarding may continue until the whole pack is used. The hands must then be played as they finally stand, even if one or both players have to hold on to some cards instead of discarding them, due to lack of replacements.

This discarding feature gives the game its name and so finely was Écarté developed that play was automatic with hands that came up to certain standards, which include the following.

Any hand containing three trump cards.
Any hand with two trumps, if it has three of another suit; or two of another suit with one a Queen.
Any hand with one trump if it has four of another suit headed by the King; or three of another suit headed by the Queen, with a Queen as odd card.
Any hand with no trump if it contains three Queens or any four picture cards.

Such hands, called *jeux de régle* represent minimum requirements and some players may go on a still lower basis, not because such hands are anywhere near sure winners, but because the odds are generally 2 to 1 or better in their favor, so they win out in the long run.

EUCHRE

Long a popular game, Euchre is best suited to four-handed play, with two teams of partners. A 32-card pack, running from Aces down to Sevens is utilized in this game, which is played as follows.

The pack is shuffled and five cards are dealt to each player. One suit is declared to be trump; and its Jack becomes the Right Bower, or highest card of the suit. Next is the Jack of the same color, or Left Bower; then the trumps run A,K,Q,10,9,8,7.

Thus Spades as trumps would rank as follows.

J♠   J♣   A♠   K♠   Q♠   10♠   9♠   8♠   7♠

Other suits would run A, K, Q, J, 10, 9, 8, 7 except for Clubs which would have no Jack.

Play normally begins with the player on the dealer's left, who leads a card. The others follow suit in rotation, until all four have played, making a trick. If unable to follow suit, a

53

player may play any card he wants. The highest card of the suit led wins the trick; but trumps take all others.

Whoever wins the first trick leads to the next; this continues until all tricks are taken. The object of each team is to take three tricks; and in some cases all five. This depends upon the manner in which the trump is *made* or chosen, according to the following rules.

Immediately after the deal, the dealer turns the next card face up on the pack. Whatever its suit, each player now has the privilege of making that suit trump, beginning with the player on the dealer's left. If he thinks his hand is strong enough for his partner and himself to win three tricks, he announces, "I order it up," which means that the dealer picks up the trump card from the pack and discards another from his hand, face down.

If the first player does not like his hand, he says, "I pass," and the choice goes to the second player. If he wants the turned up card to represent trump, he announces, "I assist," because the dealer is his partner. The result is the same. The turned up card becomes trump; the dealer picks it up and discards another.

The second player can pass if he wants to; the third player then has the same options of *ordering it up* or *passing*. The latter choice leaves it up to the dealer, who can say, "I take it up" and so on, if he thinks his hand is good enough. Otherwise, he can say, "I turn it down." In that case, he slides the turned up card under the pack and its suit is no longer a possible choice of trump.

The first player then may make another suit trump, but if his hand is weak, he can say, "I pass the making." If he passes, it goes on to the second player, then the third, and finally the dealer. If nobody cares to make a new trump, the hands are thrown in and the cards are passed along to the next dealer.

Once the turned up trump has been accepted, the play begins, as described. If the team that decided on the trump takes 3 or 4 tricks, it scores one point. Taking all five is a *march* and scores two points. If they take less than three tricks they are *euchred* and the opposing team scores two points.

During the preliminary of accepting or making the trump, each player may also announce, "I play alone." This means he has a strong hand and does not need his partner's help. So his partner lays his hand face down and play proceeds. If the man on the dealer's left has laid down his hand, the dealer's partner makes the first lead.

When playing alone, a player scores four points if he takes all five tricks; if he takes 3 or 4, he scores one point; if he takes less than three, he is euchred and the opposing team scores the usual two points.

The first team making five points wins the game. This makes scoring a simple matter. Two cards of low value can be used for this purpose, as a Two and a Three. For 1 point, cover half of the face up Two with the face down Three. For 2 points, uncover the Two completely. For 3 points, turn the Two face down and the Three face up. For 4 points, turn the Two face up and cover one spot of the Three. For 5 points spread both cards face up.

One team uses a pair of Black spot cards for scorers; the other a pair of Red cards.

Two-Handed Euchre

This is much simpler than the partnership game as there is no *playing alone* against two others. Usually the pack is reduced to 24 cards, Aces down to Nines, to produce more action. Otherwise the play is about the same.

The first player can *order up* trump to the dealer; or he may pass, letting the dealer *take it up* or pass. If both pass, each has the privilege of *making* a new trump. If that is done, the first player leads and the dealer follows.

Scoring is the same as in the regular four-handed game, but without the bonus for playing alone.

Three-Handed Euchre

Automatically included in this game is the *playing alone* feature, so a player scores three points for a *march*. In a 4-handed game a march counts 4 points, in a three-handed game a march counts 3 points. If he takes three or four tricks, he scores one point; if less than three, he is *euchred* and each of his opponents scores two points. If both reach five points or an equal number over five in the same hand, the first player to the dealer's left is the winner.

To avoid that, some players prefer the following version.

Set Back Euchre

A player, when *euchred* is *set back* two points, by having them deducted from his score. In this case, no points are given to the other players. Often a player may go *in the hole* with a score *below zero* which he must make up later. This helps to prolong the game, which is an advantage in Euchre.

Laps

Laps form another popular method. Players mark up or settle for each game won or lost; but any surplus points gained by the winner or winning team are credited as a start on the score of the next game.

FAN TAN

This name, which comes from a Chinese game played with counters, has been applied to a card game in which suits are built in sequence. Whenever builds are blocked or stopped, a player is forced to contribute a chip to the pot. Hence this game falls into a category known as *stops*.

In *Simple Fan Tan*, usually played by three to seven persons, cards are dealt around one at a time, until the pack is exhausted. It does not matter if some players each have one card more than others.

The player to the left of the dealer takes any card from his hand and places it face up in the center of the table. The next player builds on that card with the next highest card of the same suit, and others continue the build, card by card.

Thus, starting with the 3♦, the 4♦ would follow, then the 5♦, and so on. Upon reaching the K♦, the build continues with the A♦, followed by the 2♦, which in this case, would terminate the sequence. Whoever plays the final card is allowed to play a card of another suit, as a *starter* for a new sequence.

This continues until the whole pack is used up, but any time a player is stopped because he does not hold a needed card, he must put a chip in a common pool, or pot. The play then moves to the next player, who must also continue the sequence or contribute a chip.

When one player goes out by playing his final card, the others count the cards they still hold and contribute a chip for each card. The player who goes out wins the entire pot.

Popular Fan Tan or Card Dominoes

Popular Fan Tan, also known as *Card Dominoes*, is much more widely played, and is the one most people recognize as *Fan Tan*. The whole pack is dealt around and the player at the dealer's left begins by playing a Seven of any suit face up. If the man to the dealer's left can't play a Seven, he is stopped and must pay a chip, then play goes to the next man, and so on, until a Seven is played.

The next player may build upward by placing the Eight of the same suit so it overlaps the Seven on the right; or he may build downward by placing the Six of that suit so it overlaps the Seven on the left. Instead, he may place another Seven face up on the table.

Each player continues the process, either building from the Seven up to the King, or down from the Seven to the Ace. Always, play of another Seven is allowable, until no more are available. If a play is blocked, the player must put a chip in the pot, and at the finish players contribute a chip for each card that they have in hand. The one who goes out takes the pot.

Parliament

Parliament is an English form of the game, played in precisely the same way, except that the play is started by the player holding the Seven of Diamonds, who must play that card to begin. In all versions of the game, it is smart to hold *blockets*. Strategy consists of blocking your opponents, as long as possible, from running a sequence, by holding up a key card, thus forcing your opponents to chip while you get rid of your cards in the most advantageous way. (For instance, holding the 10♦ with no higher cards of that suit, so that other players are stopped from play.)

Fives or Nines

Fives or Nines is a form of Fan Tan that allows the first player to start with a Five or a Nine instead of a Seven. Whichever value is used, builds go up and down from it, as in Fan Tan. Other players must conform to the original choice; if one starts with a Five, so must the rest. Or starting with a Nine calls for Nines from then on.

In all forms of Fan Tan, the first player, or players simply lose their turn if unable to deliver the original *starter*. But after play is under way, the rule of paying one chip is invoked, whenever a player is stopped.

A player must make a play whenever possible. If he is caught holding back, he must put three chips in the pot. If he holds back on a starter by passing his turn instead of playing it, he must pay five chips each to the first player who is prevented from playing a card of higher value.

Snip, Snap, Snorem

Snip, Snap, Snorem is a game like Simple Fan Tan, beginning with any card. But instead of building upward, players add cards of the same value but in different suits. Thus the J♦ might be played first, followed by the J♥, J♣, J♠. The second card is called *Snip*, the third *Snap*, and the fourth *Snorem*. Whoever plays Snorem can immediately play a card of another value, which the other players must duplicate if they can. No chips are contributed during play, but at the finish, each pays a chip for each card he has left in his hand.

FIVE HUNDRED

This is a very popular trump game that combines features of several others and first introduced the contract features now found in Bridge. Basically there are four players, those opposite each other playing as partners; but there are variants, with two to six, as will be described.

In the basic game, 43 cards are used, consisting of the Joker, with Red Suits running A, K, Q, J, 10, 9, 8, 7, 6, 5, 4 and Black suits A, K, Q, J, 10, 9, 8, 7, 6, 5. When a suit is named trump, it runs Joker, Jack (Right Bower), Jack in suit of same color (Left Bower), Ace, King and so on down.

This gives a trump suit two more cards than normally given; while the suit of the opposite color is one card shy. For instance, with Hearts as trump, the suits would run:

Trump: Joker, J♥, J♦, ♥: A, K, Q, 10, 9, 8, 7, 6, 5, 4
Other Suits: ♦: A, K, Q, 10, 9, 8, 7, 6, 5, 4
          ♣: A, K, Q, J, 10, 9, 8, 7, 6, 5
          ♠: A, K, Q, J, 10, 9, 8, 7, 6, 5

With No-trump, which is also played in Five Hundred, all suits run normally from Ace down, with the Joker rating as the highest card in any suit the holder decides upon.

The pack is shuffled and dealt, each player receiving ten face down cards, in rounds of 3-4-3 or 3-3-4. At the end of the first round, three cards are dealt in a special pile as *widow*, though some players prefer to lay aside a single card after each round.

Players look at their hands and beginning at the dealer's left, each *passes* or makes a *bid* stating how many tricks he and his partner will guarantee to take in a stated suit. The lowest bid is Six Spades, which is worth 40, and values increase as follows.

TRUMP	6 TRICKS	7 TRICKS	8 TRICKS	9 TRICKS	10 TRICKS
Spades	40	140	240	340	440
Clubs	60	160	260	360	460
Diamonds	80	180	280	380	480
Hearts	100	200	300	400	500
No-trump	120	220	320	420	520

Each bid must be higher than the one preceding it and the highest bidder picks up the widow, adds its three cards to his hand and discards three that he does not want, without showing any of them. If all players pass, the cards are gathered and new hands are dealt by the next dealer.

In some circles, each player is allowed only one bid; in others, bidding may continue until three players have passed in succession, as in Bridge, which increases the competition. In any case, the highest bidder takes the widow and begins the play, even if he outbid his partner in the same suit.

In the play, the bidder leads any card he wants; others follow suit, unless out of it, in which case they discard from another suit, or they may trump if an ordinary suit is led. The highest card takes the trick; if trumped, the highest trump wins. The winner of each trick leads to the next.

One player gathers in the tricks for his team, turning each

packet face down and crosswise on the one below, so they can be easily counted. A team making its bid scores the amount shown on the chart; thus a successful bid of Seven Diamonds would mean 180 points.

There is no bonus for extra tricks, unless a team makes a sweep of all ten, which entitles it to a minimum of 250. Thus a bid of up to Eight Spades would count 250 for a sweep; higher bids would simply rate their normal value.

If a team fails to make its bid, that amount of the bid is deducted from its score. In every hand, the non-bidding team scores 10 points for each trick it takes. Thus a team bidding Eight Diamonds and taking only seven tricks would be scored *minus* 280, while the opposition would score *plus* 30.

The aim of the game is to reach 500. If two teams do so in the same hand, the bidding team wins. If a team goes more than 500 *in the hole* due to a loss of successive bids, it loses. By agreement, this can be set lower, as -100 instead of -500. But such a rule is essential to prevent outlandish bidding.

Another option is the inclusion of a *Nullo* bid, in which a team contracts to *lose all tricks* in a No-trump hand. This bid must be announced as Nullo and counts as 250, rating between Seven Clubs and Seven Spades in the bidding scale. A player bidding Nullo must discard the Joker if he holds it, for unless he buries it in the widow, it will take a trick.

If he does not hold the Joker, he should not bid Nullo unless his partner has passed or an opponent has bid Six or Seven No-trump. Otherwise, the Joker might be in his partner's hand, which is also fatal. A player failing to make Nullo loses 250 for his team; the opponents score 10 for each trick the bidding team takes.

Though the Joker tops any suit in No-trump, a player holding it cannot play it on another person's lead until he is out of suit. That is, the Joker is restricted as if it were a lone trump. However, a player may lead the Joker himself, naming it as a suit, and all others must follow suit if they can.

Other forms of Five Hundred follow.

Three-Handed

A very popular game, using 33 cards, consisting of Joker and four suits from Ace down to Seven. This closely resembles the standard four-handed game, but each player is *on his own* and must bid accordingly, as the other two players form a partnership against the bidder, during that hand.

The bidder scores as usual, while the other two players count their tricks singly. Each player is scored individually throughout the game. If two non-bidders are approaching 500, one may *call out* by taking a trick giving him that total. He is then the winner, unless the bidder still has a chance to reach 500 in that hand, which must then be played out, as in the four-handed game.

The Nullo bid is popular in the three-handed game as the bidder does not have to worry about a partner's holding. If he loses, the opponents each score 10 points for any trick the Nullo bidder takes.

Two players can play a modified form of the three-handed game by dealing the third hand to one side and letting it remain idle. Bidding and play proceed as usual, but with only two hands involved, the third being an unknown factor throughout.

Five-Handed

This game requires the full pack of 52 cards plus the Joker, so that each player receives the usual ten, with three for the widow. Each player is on his own, but the successful bidder is allowed to choose a partner for that hand, by one of two methods previously agreed upon.

1. The bidder calls upon anyone as partner, usually picking a player who made a high bid of his own. *2.* The bidder may call for a certain card, say the Ace of Spades, and whoever has it shows it and becomes the bidder's partner. In some circles, the card is not shown and the identity of the partner remains a mystery until the card is played. When the bidder's partner is not known, the game proves more exciting since tricks may be conceded to a *mistaken partner* and the error is not revealed until the card named by the bidder is played. This, too, should be agreed upon beforehand, one way or the other.

Six-Handed

A partnership game, with three teams of two players each; or two teams consisting of the *odd* and *even* players, counting around the table. Either way, extra cards are required in the form of two Thirteens (both Red), four Twelves and four Elevens, which rank below the face cards but above the Tens.

This makes a 63 card pack, counting the Joker, so hands and widow can be dealt as usual. Such packs may be obtained at many stores or from the manufacturer.

HEARTS

In its basic form, this exciting game is played as follows. A 52-card pack is used, values running from Ace down to Two. This applies with four players; with only three players, a Deuce is previously taken from the pack; with five players; two Deuces are removed; with six players take out ♠2, ♦2, ♣2 and ♣3. This enables the deal to come out evenly. The ♥2 is not removed.

The pack is dealt face down, preferably one card at a time. The players look at their hands and the player on the dealer's left leads any card he wants. The others follow suit if they can; if not, they discard from another suit. The highest card of the suit led takes the trick, which is turned down in front of the taker, who then leads to the next trick.

There is no trump and each player is on his own, so the play is quite simple. However, tricks do not count in a player's favor; in fact, it is generally advisable not to take them. That is because each Heart taken counts one point *against* the player taking it; hence getting rid of Hearts is the sole object of this game and frequently managed by discarding them when out of a suit led. Also, leading a low Heart often forces another player to take it with a higher Heart.

In the basic game, each hand of *Hearts* is a game in itself; hence the player with the least Hearts at the finish wins the game. If two have the same number of Hearts, they are tied. Often, chips are used in scoring or in settlement, one simple way being for each player to contribute a chip for each Heart he holds.

Thus: If A has 3 Hearts, B has 3 Hearts, C has 2 Hearts, D has 5 Hearts, A and B would each pay 3 chips and D, 5 chips to the winner, C, who would collect 11 chips in all.

With a tie, as A and B each holding 2 Hearts, with C having 3 and D having 4, C would pay 3 chips and D would pay 4, a total of 7. A and B would divide those, taking 3½ chips each. For this reason, chips of fractional value should be available; or if preferred, scores can be marked down after each game and settled later.

Some players prefer to settle on a sweepstake basis, with everybody chipping in for the exact number of Hearts he took. Such chips form a cumulative pot until a hand is played in which a player holds no Hearts at all, thus winning the whole pot. If two or more tie with no Hearts, they split the pot.

Heartsette

This name applies to a form of *Hearts,* in which the entire pack is used and dealt singly, with any extra cards, in 3, 5, 6 or 7-handed games, being laid face down as a *widow*. This batch of cards goes to the player who takes the first trick.

Normally, a player avoids this, since the widow may contain a Heart; but someone has to take the first trick, and whoever does is allowed to look at the widow without showing it to the others. This sometimes gives him an advantage in the ensuing play.

The widow feature, as well as several others, is commonly used in the modern game of Discard Hearts.

Discard Hearts

Immediately after the deal, each player takes three cards he does not want and gives them face down to the player on his right. Nobody is allowed to look at such cards until he has passed along three of his own. In Discard Hearts, individual scores are kept with each hand and the first player to reach 60 is the loser. The player with the lowest score is then declared the winner. Often, the winner is in the *minus* column when the 10♦ is used in the game.

The *Black Maria* is a name given to the Q♠, which counts as 13 Hearts against a player taking it. By passing along such cards as the A♠ or K♠, a player may lessen his chance of having to take the Black Maria. In some circles, the Q♠ must be played at the holder's first chance to get rid of it, rather than saving it to *unload* on some special opponent.

The *Minus Card* is the 10♦, which helps a player by deducting 10 points from his score. Higher Diamonds are good cards to hold in hope of *catching the ten* during play.

Taking All Points is accomplished when a player takes tricks that include *all* the Hearts, the Q♠ and the bonus 10♦. If he is able to do this, the Hearts and Black Maria go to his advantage, deducting 26 points from his score along with 10 for the minus card, or minus 36 in all. Failure to do this means that any Hearts or the Q♠ count against him. In this, and other variations of *Hearts*, a player who Takes All Points is usually paid double for each Heart.

Note: Some circles use the J♠ instead of the Q♠; or the 8♦ instead of the 10♦, etc. Extra *penalty* or *minus* cards may also be counted, if everybody is in accord. Points assigned to each may vary. In all forms of *Hearts*, penalties are important when a player revokes by failing to follow suit when he can. If he does not correct the fault immediately, he is charged with all the Hearts, as well as the Q♠ when it is a penalty card. If a player is out of cards toward the end of the hand due to a misdeal or a misplay, all remaining tricks go to him. A misdeal or misplay should be corrected, if noted, when it occurs.

Joker Hearts may be played like the simple game, or as an added attraction with Discard Hearts. In it, the Joker counts as an unusual penalty card. It ranks as a Heart, just below the J♥, so it can only be taken by the four highest Hearts A, K, Q, J. But it also is *wild*, ranking as the highest card in every other suit, so it cannot be *thrown* on any non-Heart lead or it will take the trick. The Joker counts 5 points against the player who takes it.

Auction Hearts

Auction Hearts is the basic game played with chips, but at the start each player bids for the privilege of naming the suit that is to count against the trick takers. Highest bidder must contribute that many chips to the pot, to be taken by the winner in addition to the usual pay offs in the suit named.

Domino Hearts

Domino Hearts starts with six cards dealt to each player, with the rest of the pack set face down on the table. If a player cannot follow suit, he must draw cards from the pack until he gets a needed card. When all cards have been drawn, play proceeds as usual.

When a player uses up his cards, the others simply go on

without him. If a player is left with extra cards in hand, he must add them to his tricks. Hearts are then counted and scored in the usual fashion.

Spot Hearts

Spot Hearts is a game wherein a Heart counts for face value against the player taking it: Ace is 14, King is 13, and so on down to Deuce, which is 2. There are 104 points and each hand is settled as an individual game.

Slobberhannes

A modified form of *Hearts* played with a 32-card Euchre pack, cards ranking Ace down to Seven, but with lower values removed—or added—to make the hands come out even, according to the number of players. Four is therefore the best number, but in any case, each player is on his own.

The play is exactly as in *Hearts*, but there are only four points that count against a player. They are: taking first trick, taking last trick, taking the Queen of Clubs—1 point for each; the fourth point, when it occurs, is Slobberhannes, which consists of a player being *loaded* or caught with all three.

When one player reaches 10 points, the player with the lowest score wins. As commonly played, if a player reneges by failure to follow suit, he is charged one point as penalty.

Four Jacks or Polignac

This is the French form of *Hearts* and it is played with the 32-card pack, running in value Ace down to Seven. There are up to six players in the game, and individual Sevens should be removed to make the deal come out evenly.

Instead of Hearts, the Jacks count against the player or players taking them. The Jack of Spades or Polignac, counts 2 points; the other Jacks 1 point each, or 5 points in all. The play is exactly as in *Hearts*.

When one player reaches 10 points, the player with the lowest score wins. In one popular form of the game, anyone reaching 10 points drops out, but the rest keep on until only one player has less than 10 points, and therefore wins.

MICHIGAN

A fast moving game and probably the most popular of the *stops* variety. It is played with a layout consisting of four cards taken from another pack: an Ace, a King, a Queen and a Jack of different suits as A♠, K♦, Q♣, J♥.

These are called *money cards* and before the deal begins, each player puts a stated number of chips—say five—upon whichever boodle cards he wants. There are three to seven players in the game, and the cards run in ascending value 2, 3, 4, 5, 6, 7, 8, 9, 10, J, Q, K, Ace—which is high. Suits are also important, as will be seen.

The cards are dealt face down and the dealer includes an extra hand, or *dummy*, which is the first in rotation. The deal continues until all cards have been dealt singly, as it does not matter if any players have one extra card.

The players look at their hands and if the dealer doesn't like his hand, he lays it down and takes the dummy hand instead. If he keeps his original hand, he must sell the dummy to whichever player is willing to bid highest for it, if any, such a player discards his own hand and takes the dummy.

The player at the dealer's left starts play by laying down the lowest card of any suit face up. If he can follow with more cards of that suit in sequence, he does so, as Hearts 6, 7, 8, 9. When he stops, the player holding the 10♥ plays it, and continues the sequence if he can.

Play continues until it reaches the Ace of that suit, unless it is stopped earlier, as often there is a gap in the sequence, due to a card being in the discarded dummy. After a stop, the same player may play his lowest card of another suit. If he has no other suit, play moves to his left. In the late stage of a hand, it may come clear around to him, in which case he can play the lowest of the same suit.

Suppose a player is holding ♠: 5,6,7,J,Q ♥: 10,J,K,A. He plays the 10♥, then the J♥. Another player adds the Q♥. The original player adds the K♥ and A♥. He then goes into Spades, playing 5, 6, 7. Nobody has the 8♠, but he cannot play the J♠, because it is the same suit. If the remaining players held nothing but Spades, as 2, 3, 4, 9, 10, K, A; the original player could play the J♠.

Any time a player matches a money card, he picks up the chips that are on it. This is why the player was quick to play the 10♥ and J♥ in the case above, as the J♥ is a money card. When a player goes *out* by playing his final card, he collects one chip each for all cards held by other players.

Often, nobody collects on a money card, either because it is in the dummy, or because some player goes out before another has a chance to play it. So the chips stay there until the next deal. This adds to the size of the stake and also to the interest in the game.

If a player holds back when he should have played, and the fact is discovered, he must pay a chip to every other player. Also, if he prevented another player from cashing in on a money card, he must give that player all the chips he would have won. Finally, a player committing such a fault is not allowed to cash in if he hits a money card, nor can he win by going out. Play continues until someone else' goes out and wins the hand. It pays to be careful in Michigan.

Newmarket

Newmarket is the English form of Michigan. The games are practically identical, except that in Newmarket, as originally played, the dummy hand is dead from the start, and cannot be picked up by a player. In some groups, that rule still applies with both Newmarket and Michigan.

Saratoga

Saratoga is simply another name for Michigan, but usually implies that a fixed amount should be placed on each money card, instead of letting players place it as they want.

Boodle

Boodle is the same as Michigan. The money cards are sometimes termed *boodle cards*, hence the name. Sometimes, extra boodle cards are included, as ♠: 10, J which pay off to a player who hits both in one hand.

Cross Color

Cross Color is the same as Michigan but after a player is stopped in a suit like Hearts, he must switch to a suit of the other color, namely a Black suit like Spades or Clubs. This governs a player's choice and adds some complication to the game.

Comet

Comet is an early game from which Michigan was developed. It is much the same, but instead of dealing a dummy hand, the cards are dealt evenly, and either the extras or the final round are simply discarded to serve as stops.

NAPOLEON—NAP

This is a highly popular game in England, played by 2 to 7 players, each on his own. An entire pack of 52 cards is used, running from Ace down to Two in value.

Five cards are dealt to each player. Starting at the dealer's left, each may bid a number of tricks that he intends to take — 1, 2, 3, 0, 4, 5. The *O bid*, when permitted, is called *Misére* and is played as No-trump, the bidder's purpose being to lose every trick. With other bids, the bidder names the suit he wants for trump, by leading a card of that suit to start the play.

Others follow suit if possible, or throw one from another suit. The highest card of the initial suit wins the trick. The winner leads to the next trick, from any suit, and others follow if they can. When out of that suit, a player can trump or discard as he prefers.

The bidder, if successful, receives counters from the other players according to his bid; 2 from each for a *2 bid*, etc. with Misére rating 3 counters. If he loses, he gives that many counters to each. A bid of 5 is termed a *Napoleon* and the bidder receives double, or 10, from each player—if he makes it; but only pays out 5 each if he fails.

In most circles, a later bidder is allowed to top a Napoleon by bidding *Wellington* which also means taking all five tricks, but paying or receiving double the usual number of counters. Some allow a further bid called *Blucher* which also demands a sweep to be successful, and goes triple, win or lose.

A *widow* may be used by agreement. This consists of five cards dealt in the center, face down. The first player bidding *Nap* can add the widow to his hand and discard five cards. There is no Wellington nor Blucher in this version.

PINOCHLE

This game, which is played in varied form, utilizes a special pack of 48 cards, from Ace down to Nine in each suit, with each duplicated. The Ten ranks next to the Ace in value, so the cards run downward— A, A, 10, 10, K, K, Q, Q, J, J, 9, 9.

In play, there is always a trump, so a card of that suit takes a trick when played on leads from other suits. Otherwise, the card of highest value in the led suit takes the trick. If two identical cards are played on one trick as the A◊ and the A♦, the one played first wins.

From 12 to 16 cards are dealt to each player—according to the type of game—and from these, a player can form combinations known as *melds* which he shows to the other players and by such declaration gains points toward his score.

These melds fall into the following categories:

A Trump Sequence: A, 10, K, Q, J   *150 points*

	Royal Marriage: K and Q of trumps	40 points
	Plain Marriage: K and Q of any suit	20 points
B	Pinochle: formed by J♦ and Q♠	40 points
	Double Pinochle: J♦, J♦, Q♠, Q♠	80 points
C	Four Aces in different suits	100 points
	Four Kings in different suits	80 points
	Four Queens in different suits	60 points
	Four Jacks in different suits	40 points
D	Nine of trump, called *Dix* or *Deece*	10 points

A card can be used only once in a meld of its own type; but it can be used in a meld of another type. The following is an example.

A player forms a trump sequence ♠: A, 10, K, Q, J. He cannot add the other K♠ to the Q♠ in the sequence to form a Royal Marriage as both melds are *Type A*.

However, he could add the J♦ to the Q♠ and call it a Pinochle, which is *Type B*. He could add the Q♦, Q♥, Q♣ to the Q♠ to form Four Queens, which belong in *Type C*.

Similarly, he could add the K♣ to the Q♣ to form a Plain Marriage, since the Q♣ is in a *Type C* meld and the new marriage would be *Type A*.

Since the J♦, above, is so far only in *Type B*, and the J♠ only in *Type A*, the J♣ and J♥ could be added to them to form Four Jacks, which is *Type C*.

But he could not add a second Q♠ to the present J♦, as it already forms a Pinochle, *Type B*, with a Q♠, or he would be using the J♦ twice in a meld of the same type.

There is also a special meld known as a Round House or Round Trip that applies in certain games. It is composed of four Kings and four Queens, one of each suit, which also form a Royal Marriage and three Plain Marriages, giving the player 240 points for the meld.

After declaring melds, the same cards are used in play, along

with any that were not melded. A player is credited with points
for winning specific cards, according to one of the following
schedules, each of which totals 240 points.

Original		Simplified		Popular	
Each Ace	11	Each Ace	10	Each Ace	10
Each Ten	10	Each Ten	10	Each Ten	10
Each King	4	Each King	10	Each King	5
Each Queen	3	Last Trick	10	Each Queen	5
Each Jack	2			Last Trick	10
Last Trick	10				

Procedure varies with various forms of Pinochle, so each
will be treated individually, beginning with the most popular.

Auction Pinochle

Fifteen cards are dealt to each of three players, usually by
threes, with three dealt aside as a *widow*, all cards being face
down. The players look at their hands and either pass or bid
the number of points which each thinks he can make in meld
and play.

The player at the dealer's left starts the bidding and once a
player has passed, he cannot bid again. Bidders, however, can
raise each other as often as they wish. Usually, a minimum
bid of either 250 or 300 is required; if no one will go that
high, the hands are thrown in and dealt by the next dealer.
Often, players agree to make the bidding start automatically.
The player at the dealer's left *must* bid a minimum of 300.

No suit is specified during the bidding, as the highest bidder is allowed to name it afterward. Often the size of the bid
has to do with his choice of suit; still more often, the widow
is the important factor, as it goes to the successful bidder.

Consider the following sample hand.

♦: A,A,10,K,K,J   ♠: A,K,Q,J,9   ♥: A,K   ♣: A,Q

With Diamonds as trump, the player has a meld of four Aces, 100, plus a Pinochle, 40, and a Plain Marriage in Spades, 20, for a total of 160. Its playing strength might warrant a bid of 300.

With Spades as trump, the King and Queen become a Royal Marriage, 40, and the 9♠ is worth 10 as Dix, raising the meld to 190, but lessening the playing strength. So the player would hold his choice of trump until picking up the widow.

Often, a player will bid beyond the hand's existing value in hope of *filling* some important meld from the widow. The hand shown has three such possibilities, each worth 100 points as minimum and thereby encouraging a player to go as high as 400 if necessary. The prospects are the Q♦ which would *fill* a trump sequence in Diamonds—A, 10, K, Q, J—adding 150 for a total meld of 310.

The 10♠ which would form a trump sequence in Spades, 150, but would eliminate the Royal Marriage, 40, thus adding 110 to the present 190, for a total meld of 300.

The K♣ making Four Kings, 80, plus a Plain Marriage in Clubs, 20, coming to 100. This would bring the meld up to 260, with Diamonds trump; or 290, with Spades trump.

When a player wins a bid, the widow is turned face up so all can see it. The bidder then adds the three cards to his hand and makes his meld, laying the melded cards face up on the table. They must remain there while he discards three other cards, face down.

Assume that with the sample hand, the player bid 380 and that the widow contains these cards—K♣, 10♥, J♠.

Because of the added playing strength from the J♠, he names Spades as trump and melds as follows.

A♦ A♣ A♥ A♠	Four Aces		100 points
K♦ K♣ K♥ K♠	Four Kings		80 points
Q♣	Q♠	Plain *and* Royal Marriages	60 points
J♦		Pinochle, J♦ with Q♠	40 points
	9♠	Dix, Nine of trumps	10 points

This gives him a meld of 290, while his hand still contains the following:

♠: A,10,K   ♠: J,J   ♥: 10

From these, he discards the 10♠, K♠ and 10♥, retaining the Jacks of Spades as added trump cards. Note that he has *put away* three counters worth 30 by the simplified count, or 25 if the popular count is used. Discarded widow cards go with any tricks the player takes, so he already has a nice start toward the 90 points that he must make to meet his bid of 380. He then adds the melded cards to his hand so it stands as follows:

♠: A,K,Q,J,J,9   ♦: A,A,K,J   ♣: A,K,Q   ♥: A,K

Play proceeds by the bidder leading any card he wishes to; the other two players must follow suit if possible. If a plain suit is led, and a player is out of it, he *must* trump it if he can; otherwise, he may throw off from a plain suit.

Only on the lead of a trump must the two players each play a higher trump, if they can. When a plain suit is led, the next two players must follow suit, or trump. But, if the second player trumps, the third player need not trump higher than the second player. For example, the first player plays a card in a suit in which both other players are void. If the second one trumps with a K, the third player must also trump, but he need not go higher than K.

This is often helpful to the bidder as he can force out opposing trumps by leading extra cards from an odd suit. However, the other players have a certain advantage from seeing the bidder's meld, as it enables them to appraise his losing cards.

The purpose of the opponents is to prevent the bidder from making his necessary score. To do this, they combine their efforts by throwing *counters* on each other's tricks, a process popularly styled *smearing*. They also make any leads that they feel will discommode the bidder.

Players once were required to *head* every trick that they could; that is, play higher when possible, no matter what suit happened to be led. That rule is long obsolete and now applies only when trump is led, as already stated.

As in most games, the winner of each trick leads to the next and this continues to the end of the hand. The bidder keeps his tricks in one pile, while the opponents combine theirs. The 10 points for taking the last trick may often spell the difference between a successful bid and a loss, particularly if other counters come with it.

Each hand is like a separate game and the simplest way of scoring is on a plus and minus basis, according to specified levels, using chips or marking down the score. See the following example.

A bid of	250 to 290	wins *or* loses	5 chips each
A bid of	300 to 340	wins *or* loses	10 chips each
A bid of	350 to 390	wins *or* loses	15 chips each
A bid of	400 to 440	wins *or* loses	20 chips each

This can continue with the 450 level calling for 25 chips, the 500 level for 30 chips, and so on; but in many games, boosts are faster at the higher levels.

Some jump it up to 25 at the 400 level; 35 at 450; 45 at 500. Another way is to add 5 chips for each possible bid above 400, so that 410 is 25, 420 is 30, 430 is 35, and so on.

Other players go on the basis of 250, 5 chips; 300, 10 chips; then, 350, 20 chips; 400, 30 chips; continuing thus, with a jump of 10 chips at each level. Steepest of all is the *double up* which goes: 250, 5; 300, 10; 350, 20; 400, 40; 450, 80; 500, 160. Many variations are possible; any may be used as agreed.

Often, a player may meld enough to win his bid then and there, or come so close that no play is necessary. In that case, he simply collects on his bid. Thus if he bid 330, he would take 10 chips each from his two opponents, winning 20 in all, according to the simple form of payment.

If he has overbid his hand and sees that he cannot make his bid or that the risk is too great, the bidder can *go bate*, admitting that he has failed and is beaten. *Go bate* or *go bait* is a term used when a bidder plays the hand and loses. He must pay double—having played and lost. When a player takes the widow and realizes he has overbid and can't make the hand, he simply concedes the loss of game by throwing in his cards, refusing to play because he doesn't want to pay double. In that case, he would give 10 chips to each of his two opponents, losing 20 in all. Often a bidder prefers this out.

If a hand is played and lost, the bidder must pay double. Thus if he bid 330 and only made a 320 score, each of his two opponents would receive 20 chips, the bidder losing 40 in all. Usually, the opponents insist on playing a hand through if there is even the slightest chance of stopping the bidder; but quite often, a bidder will throw in a doubtful hand.

This is specially true when playing *Spades Double*. This is an almost universal rule in Auction Pinochle. By it, a bid in Spades means that all payments are doubled, win or lose. Thus a player bidding 330 and declaring Spades trump would win 20 chips from each opponent, or 40 in all.

However, if he simply *concedes* and throws in his hand without naming trump, his loss would only be 10 to each opponent or 20 chips in all. As a result, it is often good policy to bid high on a hand that has possibilities in Spades, banking on improvement from the widow.

If a bidder plays and loses after bidding Spades, he pays double for losing, at the double rate for Spades, or 40 chips to each opponent. This leads to close calculation when a choice of suit is involved. In the example given earlier, where a bidder could have named either Diamonds or Spades, he might prefer Diamonds as trump rather than risk a double loss in Spades by stretching it too far.

Hearts Triple is a modern innovation which, as its name implies, means triple stakes whenever Hearts is declared trump. A Heart bid, played and lost, can be a severe jolt to the bidder. By winning a 330 bid in Hearts, he would receive 30 chips from each opponent or 60 in all; declaring Hearts and losing the bid, he would give each 60 chips or 120 in all. Hearts Triple should be included in the game only by previous agreement.

Additional players may be included in a game of Auction Pinochle, but only three are active in each hand. With four players, one acts as dealer but does not participate. After the hand, the deal moves along to the next player, who simply deals to the others and leaves himself out during that deal.

With five players, two are dealt out, namely the dealer and the player to his left. This continues around the table, with three active and two inactive players during each hand.

All players figure in the scoring; however, if the bidder wins an ordinary 330 bid, he would collect 30 chips, 10 from each of the other players in a four-handed game; or 40 chips in a five-handed game. This increases the stakes in Spades double and Hearts triple proportionately.

Many veteran Pinochle players regard the four-handed game with dealer out as the ideal form of Auction Pinochle.

Two-Handed Pinochle

This differs considerably from Auction Pinochle, being practically a game in itself. The melds are the same, but they are progressive and are made singly, during the course of play, which also has its own individual features.

The dealer, A, deals twelve cards each to another player, B, and himself, either by threes or fours. He turns up the next card and inserts it partly beneath the pack, which stays face down. The face up card is the trump, and if it is the Dix, Nine, the dealer promptly marks up 10 points as a start towards his score.

The non-dealer, B, leads any card, and A plays any card he wants. He does not have to follow suit or trump at this point. The usual rule holds, however, as to taking the trick. B wins it unless A plays a higher card in that suit, or trumps a lead from an ordinary suit.

Whoever wins the trick can then meld if he has a suitable combination in his hand. Whether or not he melds, he draws the top card from the pack to bring his hand up to 12 cards. The other player does the same and the one who won the trick makes another lead. This continues, play by play, meld by meld, draw by draw.

Melded cards are left face up on the table, but they may be played at any time, instead of playing from the hand. This enables a player to hold onto cards needed for later melds.

If a player has a Dix, he may meld it by sliding it face up under the pack and picking up the trump card showing there. This is done with the second Dix, though in that case, the player merely has to show it, rather than exchange one Dix for the other. A Dix can be exchanged after a winning trick, and a single meld be put down at the same time. The last card drawn from the pack will be the face up Dix.

At that point, each player gathers up his meld and from there on, play follows the standard pattern. Whatever the trick-winner leads, the other player must follow suit if he can. Otherwise, he must trump; if out of trump, he can discard from an odd suit. Any trump lead must be overtrumped.

The *counter* cards are added up, including 10 for the last trick, and these totals are added to each player's individual meld. The original count is often used in Two-Handed Pinochle, but the players may agree upon some other. The deal then goes to Player B. More hands are played until one player reaches 1000 and becomes the winner.

A running score is kept by one player and by referring to

it, a player can usually tell when he has taken enough counters to reach the 1000 mark. He can declare out and win the game right there, unless a count proves him to be short, in which case he loses. Or if both players agree, nobody wins if both reach 1000, and the game is extended to 1250, then 1500, etc., until one wins cleanly.

Special rules apply to the melding in this game. Not only must they be made singly; a meld, to be valid, requires a new card from the hand to complete it.

Thus if a player melds four Kings for 80 and four Queens for 60, he cannot marry any of the Kings and Queens, so 140 is the limit of his meld. His proper course is to meld four Kings: 80, a Royal Marriage: 40, a Plain Marriage: 20, then another Plain Marriage: 20. He can then add the fourth Queen: 60, making a total of 220. Or if he has an odd King or Queen, he can use it to complete the last marriage.

Some players allow the Round House, four Kings and Queens, to be scored as a complete meld of 240, as in the auction or three-handed game. This is fair enough, as a player very rarely has all eight cards available at once.

The following is *always* allowable in the two-handed game. If a player makes a Royal Marriage as: K♠ and Q♠ for 40 points, he can later add the A, 10, J of trump and score 150 for the sequence. If, however, he melds the A, 10, K, Q, J first, which he may be forced to do when the *draw* is getting short, he cannot remove the K, Q from the sequence and declare it as a marriage later.

In the original game, a meld of double Pinochle was allowed; namely J♦, J♦, Q♠, Q♠, for 80 points. By the same token, a player could first meld J♦ and Q♠ for 40 points; then later add the second J♦ and Q♠ and call it double for 80 points more.

Another custom was to regard double Pinochle as a special meld that could only be made *all at once* for a score of 300 points. Today, most players simply count each Pinochle as a

40 meld of its own, so any reversion to the old rules should be mutually understood before the game.

Generally, players are allowed to meld a Dix along with another meld. Thus, a player could meld the K♣ and Q♣ for 20 while melding the Nine of trump for 10. But in such a meld, the trump picked up by the Dix cannot be used until later. Also, when a Dix is exchanged for another trump, that trump can definitely be used immediately in a meld. For example: if Hearts are trump, a 9 could be exchanged for a Queen and the Queen could be used to meld a Royal Marriage with a King from the hand. The double transaction scores 50 points.

Bezique

This is the two-handed game from which Pinochle was derived. Its two-handed form is still extensively played, often in places where Pinochle is unheard. A 64-card pack is used, running A, 10, K, Q, J, 9, 8, 7 with all cards duplicated. Melds are made and scored as in Two-Handed Pinochle, with these exceptions.

Trump sequence— A, 10, K, Q, J counts 240. The Seven of trump, not the Nine counts 10. The J♦, Q♠ combination is called a *Bezique* and scores 40, double Bezique— J♦, J♦, Q♠, Q♠ is 500. Though a double Bezique is held in hand, the player may take the opportunity to score more points by first melding a single Bezique for 40 after 1 trick, and a double Bezique for 500 later, thus scoring 540 points in total.

The reason for the higher values in Bezique is that eight cards are dealt to each player, making melds more difficult. After the players' hands are dealt the next card is turned up as trump and play proceeds as in Two-Handed Pinochle, with the following exceptions.

Only Aces or Tens count in scoring. They are called

Brisques and are worth 10 each, making 160, with the last trick as 10, for a total of 170 points to be taken in play.

Melds are made after taking a trick, and only one may be declared, but the player can lay down others as futures, say— A, 10, K, Q, J of trump, saying "Score 40 for Royal Marriage with 250 to score." Or he could lay down—J♦, K♠, Q♠ saying: "Score 40 for Bezique and 20 to score for Marriage." Inasmuch as a player can declare only one meld after each winning trick, there would be no purpose in declaring futures. It is a fact that a player having a high trump sequence may first meld the Royal Marriage to score 40, and take a chance that he will win another trick so he can then lay down the A, 10, J to score 250 more for a total of 290. But, if he puts cards down for futures his opponent can often take measures to stop a further meld, especially late in the game. Therefore, a player with scoring possibilities in hand would prefer not to tip his hand.

Cards may be played from the meld, but any still to be scored must be retained, or their score will be sacrificed. However, the player does not have to add new cards from his hand to form new combinations; he can score any that may show, provided of course, that he has just won a trick.

These rules are not adamant, as Bezique is an old game and has experienced changes and local variations during the years. In play, however, anything may be led, thrown or trumped, until the pack has all been drawn. Then, as in Pinochle, the rules of following suit and trumping must be fulfilled; with Bezique each player has eight cards during this final play.

The high value of 500 given to *double Bezique* accounts for the old score of 300 for *double Pinochle* sometimes used by Pinochle players. But whereas it remains an integral part of Bezique—due to the greater difficulty of the double meld —it is no longer a part of Pinochle.

Sixty-Four Card Pinochle

Sixty-Four Card Pinochle should not be confused with Be-zique. In this game, a Bezique pack of 64 cards is used, with the Seven of trump serving as the Dix. But the melding, playing and scoring all conform to the accepted rules of Two-Handed Pinochle, except that in the more popular version of the 64-card game, each player is dealt a hand of sixteen cards.

This increases the melding opportunities and lengthens the final stage of play, where any melded cards still on the table are taken back into the hand.

PIQUET

This famous French game is for two players using a 32-card pack with values running from Ace down to Seven. Other games have stemmed from it, and two of its features, the *draw* and ways of hand evaluation, could well have inspired our modern Poker.

Each player is dealt 12 cards by twos or threes and the rest of the pack, 8 cards, is laid face down. The first player, A, looks at his hand and discards 1 to 5 cards in a face down heap, drawing the same number from the pack to replace them.

The dealer, B, does not have to draw, but can, if he wishes, draw up to the number still remaining in the pack. This may be as few as 3 or as many as 7, according to the size of A's draw. B must also discard before drawing.

The purpose of the draw is to improve the hand in hope of winning certain declarations and scoring as a result. To clarify this, suppose that after the draw the two hands stand as follows:

	A		**B**
Diamonds	A 10 9 8 7	Diamonds	K Q J
Clubs	Q 8	Clubs	A K J 10 9
Hearts	A Q	Hearts	K J
Spades	A K Q	Spades	J 7

Declarations are first made by Player A; then confirmed or disputed by Player B. They go as follows.

Point is won by the player with the most cards of a single suit. A states how many he has, in this case five, in Diamonds. If B has less in his longest suit, he says, "Good," and A scores the number of cards he announced. If B has more he says, "Not good," and B scores *point* according to the number in his suit.

If both have the same number, they count the spots on their cards; Ace, 11; face cards, 10 each; others according to spots. If either has a higher count, he wins *point;* if both are the same, no *point* is scored.

In the example, A has five cards in Diamonds; B has five in Clubs. A's add up to 45 (11, 10, 9, 8, 7) while B's add up to 50 (11, 10, 10, 10, 9). B scores 5 for point.

Sequence is the next declaration. A announces the number of cards in his longest sequence, in this case, "Four," consisting of ♦: 10,9,8,7. B says "Good," if he has less; "No good," if he has more. If he says, "Equal," the sequence with the highest top card wins. In this case, if B held ♣: J,10,9,8 he would beat A's run. If the sequences prove actually equal, neither player scores.

A sequence must contain at least three cards. Each card scores 1 and if there are more than three, the player scores 10 extra regardless of how many additional cards the sequence contains. Also, the player winning sequence scores for any other sequence in his hand.

In the example, A scores 14 for the winning sequence ♦ 10,9,8,7 and 3 points for an additional sequence ♠: A,K,Q. B has two 3-card sequences, but they do not count, as he lost. A scores 17 for sequence.

Quatorze is the next declaration. Here, the player is aiming for Four of a Kind—cards all alike in value, scoring 1 each with 10 for a fourth, making 14, the meaning of a quatorze in French. If he has no *Fours* he can declare *Threes* and, in either case, the set with higher values wins. Also, the winner scores any additional sets of *Threes* or *Fours;* but only Aces, Kings, Queens, Jacks and Tens score.

In the example, A declares, "Three Aces," hoping that they are high, so he can score 3 for Aces and another 3 for that many Queens. But B says, "No good," and therewith declares, "Four Jacks," for 14 and, "Three Kings," for 3 more. So A's *trios* do not count. B scores 17 for quatorze.

That ends the immediate declarations and the play begins. A, being non-dealer, leads any card he wants, scoring 1 for each trick led, whether or not he wins it, so he is sure of 12 more. B must follow suit if he can, the high card winning; otherwise, he discards from another suit, losing the trick. The winner of each trick leads to the next, and every time B wins a trick, he scores 1 for winning and 1 for leading, thus *keeping up* with A.

In addition, the player taking the last trick scores 1 for it; and if either player wins more than six tricks, he scores 10 *for the cards.* At the end of the hand, the cards are gathered and A makes the next deal. Scores are added during successive hands and the first player to reach 100 wins the game.

There are also certain bonus declarations which may occur.

Carte Blanche consists of a hand containing no face cards, Kings, Queens or Jacks. Such a hand takes precedence over all other declarations. The player shows his cards and scores 10 for carte blanche. The usual draw and declarations follow.

Repique is scoring 30 points or more through declarations before the other player scores any. Thus A might score 5 for *point;* 15 for a *quint sequence,* five cards; and 14 for quatorze, as—J, J, J, J giving him a 34 total. Because of this, he receives 60 more for repique, enabling him to win the game in a single hand, as first player.

Pique can be scored only by the first player, as it consists of reaching 30 through declarations and play, against the other player's 0. Thus A with 5 for *point*, 17 for *sequence* and 6 for two *trios* would have a start of 28. By taking the first two tricks, he would add 1 each, so the score would stand A: 30; B: 0. For *pique* the player adds 30 to his score; so it would be A: 60; B: 0.

Capot is taking all twelve tricks. The player doing so already gets 10 for taking the majority. For capot he scores 30 more.

During declarations of play, a player may declare *out* as soon as his score reaches 100. Many close games may be decided in that fashion.

PITCH

Older forms of Pitch are known under various names, including *Seven Up* and *High-Low-Jack,* both of which describe the scoring method. Other modern versions have been developed, and will be described in order. All have the following basis.

A pack of 52 cards is used, with suits running from Ace down to Two, in customary value. There are two to seven players and each is dealt six cards face down, usually twos or threes. One player has the privilege of naming trump, and leads to the first trick, always opening with a lead of trump, which is compulsory on that trick only.

Other players follow suit if possible, otherwise they may discard. However, when a non-trump is led—which is allowable after the first trick—a player may trump if he wants. The highest card of the suit led wins the trick, except when an ordinary suit lead is trumped; then the highest trump takes it. A player winning a trick has the next lead.

Taking tricks is merely incidental to the real aim, which is to score special points, four in number, which are rated as follows:

HIGH: Holding the highest trump card
LOW: Holding the lowest trump card
JACK: Taking the Jack of trump in play
GAME: Taking in the biggest amount in *counters,* which may be of any suit, rating each Ace as 4, King as 3, Queen as 2, Jack as 1, Ten as 10.

In *Simple Pitch,* the player to the dealer's left names the trump, often picking his strongest suit, but sometimes basing his choice on whether he holds an Ace for High or a Two for Low—as either can be shown for a sure point, since only the cards in actual play figure in the scoring of that hand.

The deal then moves one player to the left, another hand is played, and so on, until someone reaches a score of 7 points and thereby becomes winner. If more than one player goes out in the same hand, their points are counted in the following order: High, Low, Jack, Game—to determine the winner.

In any hands where the Jack is not dealt, it does not figure as a point. In counting Game, if two players have the same amount in *counters,* the Game point is eliminated.

As an option rule, Low may be scored by the player taking a trick containing the Low card of that hand, instead of the point being scored by the player who shows Low. That is not common in Simple Pitch, where the showing of Low is a time-honored tradition. It is the usual thing, though, in the modern game of Auction Pitch.

Auction Pitch

In Auction Pitch, players bid for the privilege of naming trump. Each player may pass, or make a bid of 1, 2, 3 or 4 points, providing his bid is higher than the one preceding it. If agreed upon before the start of play, the dealer can be the exception, if he bids the same as the bidder before him, the dealer wins the bid. There is only one opportunity to bid around.

Winning the bid means worse than nothing; however, if the bidder fails to make his required points, he loses the amount he bid. If he goes below zero, a circle is put around his score, showing it to be that much *in the hole*. He must make up such minus points before entering the plus column.

Smudge

Smudge has a special rule, now usually part of Auction Pitch, whereby a player bidding and making *four* goes out automatically, becoming the immediate winner, unless he happened to be in the hole, in which case he scores 4 points. Many groups allow a non-bidder to score a Smudge for taking 4 points, a very good rule, as it means scoring a *slam* against a strong hand. This, however, should be agreed upon beforehand.

Similarly, the winning score can be made higher than 7 points, to allow players more chance to recuperate after being set back in bids. A total of 11 points is usual, but some go to 21. This should also be predetermined.

The rule of scoring a point by taking Low instead of merely showing it, is customary in modern Auction Pitch, as it encourages higher bidding. It, too, should be specified, although it is practically standard, except in a game with only two players. In such a game, Low is always scored by the player who holds it.

A bid of *two* is usually the lowest allowed, and if all players pass, there is a new deal. Play is the same as in Simple Pitch, with the bidder making the first lead, to declare trump. Other players score whatever points they make, but if the bidder and another player go out in the same hand, the bidder wins.

Set Back

Set Back is another name for Auction Pitch, so-called because the bidder is *set back* whenever he loses.

The Joker may be added to Auction pitch—either as a higher trump than the Ace, or a lower trump than the Two. Its status should be fixed beforehand, but either way, it does not rate as High or Low. The player taking it scores an extra point. Thus the points become High, Low, Jack, Joker, Game—five in all.

Seven Up

Seven Up, the forerunner of Pitch, more often played as a two-handed game, but three can play; and also four in partnership—two against two. Six cards are dealt to each and the next is turned up as a trump. If the non-dealer accepts it, he makes the first lead, which may be in any suit, not just trump.

If the non-dealer doesn't want it, the dealer can accept it, by giving the non-dealer a free point. The non-dealer then leads in any suit. If the dealer doesn't want it, he deals three more cards to the non-dealer and himself, and turns up another trump.

If this trump is the same suit as before, he repeats the deal until another suit turns up as trump. Both players then discard all extra cards, reducing their hands to six cards each, and the non-dealer opens play as described. If neither likes the new trump, they can throw in their hands, and the dealer makes a new deal.

In case the dealer turns up a Jack on the original deal, he scores an automatic point. The same applies if he turns up a Jack as the new trump. Otherwise, the play follows the original rule: taking High, 1 point; taking Jack, 1 point; holding

Low, 1 point; scoring Game, 1 point. The first to reach 7 points is the winner, as the name Seven Up implies.

Shasta Sam

This game resembles Seven Up in that two players are involved, six cards are dealt to each, and the next card is turned up as trump. The non-dealer immediately leads any card he wishes, and from then on, the game follows a distinct pattern.

Whoever wins the first trick, draws a card from the top of the face down pack; then the other player draws a card. This goes on, trick by trick, each player replenishing his hand after each play, until the pack is used up. Then the remaining cards are played out.

As usual the points are High, Low, Jack and Game, but since the whole pack is used, Ace is always High and the Two is Low, counting for the player who takes it in a trick. Jack also counts for whoever takes it. Game consists of 80 *counters* and if tied, neither player wins the point.

The first to score 7 points is the winner, though that can be extended by agreement.

California Jack

California Jack is an earlier form of Shasta Sam and the two are identical except for one feature. In California Jack the pack is turned face up, so that each player sees the card that will be drawn by the winner of the trick.

This has a strong bearing on the play, often causing a player to throw away a trick rather than draw an undesirable card. In either version, the player taking the first trick draws the trump card showing on top of the pack.

Pedro

This includes different versions of a game similar to Auction Pitch, but with more points involved, making the bidding much stronger. The usual points of High, Low, Jack, Game: count 1 each, but Game is simply the Ten of trumps, all other counters being eliminated. Other trumps have special values, and all points, Low included, go to the player who takes them during play.

In Pedro of the simplest form, there is one extra point card, the Five of trumps, called Pedro, which gives the taker 5 points. Each hand, therefore, has a potential of 9 points. The player who first reaches 21 is the winner.

Pedro Sancho

In Pedro Sancho, the Nine of trumps, called Sancho, is also a point card, worth 9 in itself. Each hand has a potential of 18 points and the player who first takes 50 is the winner.

Dom Pedro

In Dom Pedro, the three of trumps, called *Dom*, is worth 3 points, when taken in play. The Joker is added to the pack and is worth 15 points to the taker. It ranks as a trump, just below the Two, but is not considered as Low. The player first reaching 100 is the winner.

Snoozer is a nickname given to the Joker, and therefore is sometimes applied to mean the game of Dom Pedro itself.

If two players both go out in the same hand, their points are counted in the following order to see which first reaches the required total: High, Low, Jack, Game (Ten), Three, Five, Nine, Joker. This order applies in all versions, simply eliminating any point cards not used. If any point card fails to appear during play, it is not scored in that hand.

POKER

Originally known as Bluff, modern Poker has many forms, all based on the early game, so its description will help clarify the rest. Five cards are dealt to each player and starting at the dealer's left, each can either *pass* or *open* the betting by placing chips in the center pot.

From then on, each player may *call*, by meeting the amount already bet; or he may *raise*, by adding extra chips; or he may *drop* from the betting entirely, throwing his hand face down. When all bets have been called, there is a *showdown* in which the hands are compared and the one with the highest combination according to an accepted schedule, is the winner of the pot.

The element of bluff occurs when a player raises a bet on a weak hand, forcing out players with stronger hands who think he has them beaten. So the higher the stakes, the greater the opportunity for bluffing as opponents may *drop* rather than *stay* unless they have very strong hands.

Hands are valued according to the following combinations

which are accompanied by the approximate chances of being dealt such hands. A 52 card pack is used, running A, K, Q, J, 10, 9, 8, 7, 6, 5, 4, 3, 2; the Ace is sometimes rated low as well as high. Suits figure in special hands—as described—but no suit takes precedence over another.

ROYAL FLUSH ♠: A,K,Q,J,10
The top five cards in any one suit. Chance: 1 out of 65,000.

STRAIGHT FLUSH ♦: J,10,9,8,7
Five cards of the same suit in sequence. If two players hold such hands, the one with the highest card wins. The lowest possible Straight Flush is a Five High—♣: 5,4,3,2,A—with the Ace counting as low card. Chance: 1 out of 65,000.

FOUR OF A KIND A♠,A♣,A♦,A♥,9♠
Four Aces, the highest possible set of four, wins over any other fours. The odd card has no significance. Chance: 1 out of 4000.

FULL HOUSE J♦,J♠,J♥,4♣,4♦
Three cards of one value, two of another. Hand with the highest three wins over any other Full. Chance: 1 out of 700.

FLUSH K♠,9♠,8♠5♦,2♦
J♦,10♦7♦,4♣,3♣
J♣,10♣,6♣,5♠,3♠
Five cards of the same suit, but not in numerical order. Flush with the highest card wins. If two have high cards of the same value, the next card rates high and so on. Chance: 1 out of 500.

STRAIGHT A♥,K♣,Q♦,J♣,10♠
9♠,8♣,7♣,6♦,5♠
5♠,4♦,3♠,2♣,A♦
Five cards in numerical order, but with mixed suits. An Ace high Straight is called a Broadway and beats all others, as a Straight is determined by its high card, lowest possible Straight is a Five high with Ace counting low. Chance of any Straight: 1 out 250.

THREE OF A KIND   9♥,9♠,9♣ K♣,4♦

As the name implies, three cards of the same numerical value, with two of different denominations. With two such hands, the one with the highest set of Triplets wins. Chance: 1 out of 50.

TWO PAIR   A♦,A♣ 9♥,9♦ 5♦
                                   J♠,J♦ 8♣,8♦ 7♦
                                   J♥,J♣ 6♦,6♥ Q♣
                                  10♦,10♥ 4♣,4♥ K♣
                                  10♠,10♣ 4♦,4♠ Q♥

Two Pair of different denominations, with an extra card of another value. If two hands or more contain Two Pair, the one with the highest pair wins. If the top pairs are tied, the hand with the higher second pair wins. If the Two Pairs are identical, the player with the higher odd card wins. Chance: 1 out of 20.

PAIR   K♥,K♦ 5♣,4♣,2♦
                                   J♥,J♦ Q♣,9♣,5♦
                                   J♠,J♥ Q♦,8♠,6♦

Two of a Kind in numerical value, with three of different denominations. If more than one hand has a Pair—as often happens— the highest Pair wins. If tied, highest odd card wins. Chances of a Pair: 1 out of 2.667.

NO PAIR   A♦,K♦,Q♠,J♠,9♣
                                   Q♥,9♦,7♦,5♣,3♣
                                   7♥,5♠,4♠,3♦,2♣

A hand with no two cards of the same value, with more than one suit represented. Highest card denotes the winner of several such hands; if high cards are the same, second highest, and so on. The highest possible No Pair and the lowest possible are both shown here. Normally, an Ace cannot be rated as a low card in such hands.

Chances as stated refer to possibilities of receiving such hands in the deal of five cards, and are therefore important in calculating prospects of other players.

Other combinations are used in various types of poker as well as freak games. Such special hands follow.

Besides the standard hands already listed, there are other combinations, some of which are widely accepted in certain areas of the country. They are all optional, so any group of players has the privilege of naming anything they want.

Big Bobtail: a four-card Straight Flush, with any odd fifth card as—Q♥, J♥, 10♥, 9♥, A♠. Rates just below Four of a Kind.

Blaze: All picture cards as—K♥, K♠, K♦, Q♣, J♠ or Q♠, Q♦, J♣, J♥, K♣. Rates just below a Full House. An actual Full House or Four of a Kind composed of all picture cards would be rated normally.

Big Dog: Ace high, Nine low of mixed suits, as— A, Q, J, 10, 9. Ranks just below a Flush.

Big Cat: King high, Eight low, of mixed suits, as— K, Q, J, 9, 8. Ranks just below a Big Dog.

Little Dog: Seven high, Deuce low of mixed suits, as— 7, 6, 5, 3, 2. Ranks just below a Big Cat.

Around the Corner Straight: A Straight with Four, Three, Deuce as high, continuing with King, Queen, Jack, below Ace, as— 4, 3, 2, A, K; 3, 2, A, K, Q; 2, A, K, Q, J. These rate below other Straights.

Skip or Dutch Straight: Alternating cards of mixed suits in sequence as— K, J, 9, 7, 5 or 10, 8, 6, 4, 2. Just below a Straight.

Kilter: The lowest Skip, running 9, 7, 5, 3, A.

Pelter or Skeet: A hand of mixed suits with a Nine, a Five, a Deuce, and other cards separating them, as— 9, 8, 5, 4, 2 or 9, 7, 5, 3, 2. Just below a Kilter.

Little Bobtail: Three cards toward a Straight Flush as— J♦, 10♦, 9♦, K♣, 5♠. Just below Three of a Kind.

Four Flush: Four cards of one suit, with an odd, as— 8♦, 6♦, 3♦, 2♦, 9♠. Valued just above a Pair in some games of Five Card Stud. In others, below a Pair, but better than an Ace high hand.

Draw Poker

For many years, Draw Poker has been regarded as the standard game, as it is simply an extension of the original form, utilizing an added feature called the *draw*.

The game is usually played by three to seven players. Each puts an *ante* in a *pot* in the center of the table. This ante consists of a specified number of chips.

Cards are dealt singly to each player, who may *pass* until someone *opens*. After that, players *drop, call,* or *raise,* as in the original game, until the totals are equal. If all players pass, the deal moves to the next man on the left, who puts up an additional ante.

If only one player stays, he automatically wins the pot, without even disclosing his hand. If two or more stay, they do not show their hands, until after each has made a *draw*. This consists of a player discarding any cards he does not want, and having others dealt to replace them.

Discards are made face down, and if the player is satisfied with his hand, he may *stand pat*, which means that he draws no cards at all. After the draw, betting is resumed. The player who opened can *bet* or *check the bet*, giving the betting privilege to the next active player to his left.

Once a bet is made, each succeeding player may call, raise or drop, as usual. After all bets have been checked or called, there is a showdown, and the player with the highest hand wins the pot.

Jackpots or Jacks or Better

Jackpots, also called Jacks or Better, is the form of Draw Poker favored in most circles. In such a game, a player must have at least a Pair of Jacks in order to open. If he drops or

wins the hand without opposition, he must show a pair of
Jacks or something better, to prove he had openers.

Sometimes a player *splits* his openers, say by discarding a
King from a Pair, in order to go after a higher hand like a
Straight of Flush. So he should keep his discard handy, to
show his openers if required.

Since a Pair of Jacks is a better than average hand, there
are times when nobody can open, so the deal moves along.
This requires another ante, increasing the size of the pot.
Players are not compelled to open, so a player *under the guns*
at the dealer's left may sometimes throw in a hand containing
a Pair of Jacks, or even a higher Pair.

All this swells the pot with further antes, which is the main
purpose of Jackpots. If so agreed, the rule can be made
progressive. After passing a hand, the next requires a Pair of
Queens, or better; then Kings, and finally Aces. The requirement can even be pushed up to Two Pair, if desired. Most
groups, however, prefer to stay with simple Jackpots.

In games where a player can open on anything, some
groups go by the rule that a player must open or drop, rather
than being allowed to pass and come back later. In Jackpots,
the rule of *pass and back in* is customary. Thus, any player is
able to stay in the face of Jacks or Better, regardless of his
position at the table.

The Draw

The draw is the great feature of Draw Poker and not only
enables a player to improve his hand to the status of a winner, but may help him to bluff opponents, by giving them a
false idea of his actual holdings. The usual procedures and
prospects are as follows.

A *Five Card Draw* is made when a player has practically
nothing in his hand. He simply wants a new hand, hoping to
do better. But whatever he gets, he is stuck with, as there will

be no further chance for improvement. Usually, such hands are thrown in and forgotten. With some groups, five card draws are not allowed.

A *Four Card Draw* is made on the strength of one high card, as an Ace or a King, which at least is a start to a better hand. But chance of matching the high card for a Pair is only about 1 out of 4, with chance of anything better about the same as on the original deal. With some groups, four card draws are not allowable.

A *Three Card Draw* is usually made in hope of improving a Pair, which the player retains while discarding three odd cards. Chance of such improvement is about 1 out of 3½.

As a desperation draw, a player may hold two unmatched cards, but even if they are high, as Ace and King, his chance of getting a high Pair is less than 1 in 2½, with little hope of anything higher.

A *Two Card Draw* is often made in hope of improving Three of a Kind which the player already holds. Chances of such improvement are a little better than 1 out of 10, and when an improvement is made chances are 2 out of 3 that it will be a Full House rather than Four of a Kind.

Many players will hold a Pair and an odd card, or *kicker* while making a two card draw. Chances of improving the Pair are almost as good as with a three card draw, particularly if the kicker is an Ace or King, which may produce a high Two Pair. Such a two card draw also has a bluff value, as opponents may think the player holds Three of a Kind.

Drawing two cards to an open-end Straight Flush ◆: Q, J,10—offers about 1 out of 12 chances of making a Straight or a Flush, with a Straight Flush a very remote prospect.

A *One Card Draw* is the only way of improving Two Pair. It allows about a 1 out of 12 chance of making a Full House.

With four parts toward an open-end Straight—10♥, 9◆, 8◆, 7♣—a player has 1 out of 6 chances of *filling* the Straight — J, 10, 9, 8, 7 or 10, 9, 8, 7, 6—so it is often worthwhile. An *inside* Straight—Q♠, J♣ 10♠, 8♥—offers only 1 out of 12 chances, so is rarely worth the try.

A *fourflush* with four cards of the same suit—♦: Q,9,7,3 —is a better bet than an *open-end* Straight, as the chance of catching a fifth card is 1 out of 5, and a Flush beats a Straight.

Many players draw only one card when holding Three of a Kind. Chance of improving is about 1 out of 12, almost as good as a two card draw. Drawing one card makes the hand look like two Pair, or a possible Straight or Flush, which may fool an opponent into betting badly.

With Four of a Kind, a player often draws one card for similar reasons, as it looks as though he is trying to improve a hand which is actually as good as it can be.

Standing Pat is necessary with a Straight, a Flush, a Full House, or a Straight Flush, as the player has no card that he can throw away. It is often advisable to stand pat on Four of a Kind, as opponents may think the hand is in a lesser category.

Occasionally, a player will stand pat on Two Pair, figuring that it makes his hand look stronger, and that the chance of getting a Full House from a one card draw is too small to matter.

Bluffing may be carried to any extreme a player wants. He can stand pat on a *nothing* hand if he thinks it will scare other players into dropping out. The bigger the stakes, the more the chance to bluff, as a hand looks strong when backed with plenty of chips.

Limits are customary in the great majority of Poker games, so a player must bet accordingly. Usually two amounts are stated, as 5-10 or 5-25, which may refer to chips, cents, dollars, or *what have you*. The first figure represents the lowest bet, the last figure, the highest.

Usually, the first figure is also the ante. So in *Five-Ten* Poker, each player would put up 5 units, except in games where the dealer antes for all, that being a simpler way to handle it. In the play, each person would bet or raise either 5 or 10 units, as in-between amounts—5, 6, 7, 8, 9—are inconvenient. In some, as *Five-Twenty-five*, bets and raises would run 5, 10, 15, 20, 25.

Sometimes only the minimum bet is allowed before the draw, and this has led to the fixing of three units, as 5-10-25, meaning that the game is 5-10 before the draw, and 10-25 afterward. If desired, it can be 5-10 before and 5-25 after. All these things are fixed by agreement.

About the cheapest form of Poker is *penny ante*, which operates on a 1M basis, pennies often being used instead of chips. In some games, everyone antes 1M and the limits are 1M to 5M, with anything in between. In contrast, some groups play 1 to 5 or 1 to 10 with dollars as the units instead of cents. Poker is that flexible.

Roodles, also known as *Whangdoodles*, is a term referring to a round of play at double stakes, or more. Often, by agreement, this follows any hand won by a Full House or better, such a hand being popularly styled a whangdoodle. The round consists of a deal by every player until it reaches the one who dealt the whangdoodle. The roodles end before the deal.

Five Card Stud

This is the original form of *Stud Poker* from which several other versions have developed. Ordinarily, there is no ante in Five Card Stud, though this is optional. In Stud, all cards are kept on the table, none being taken up into the players' hands. As many as ten players can participate comfortably in Five Card Stud.

Two cards are dealt to each player, a *hole card*, face down, and an *upcard*, face up. Each player is allowed to look at his hole card. The player with the highest up card must either open or drop, which in Stud is called *folding* because he turns down his upcard. If two players are tied for high card, the one nearest to the dealer's left must open, or fold. If he drops out, then it is up to the next man to his left to open, no matter how low an upcard he shows.

Once the pot is opened, succeeding players can fold, call or raise. This continues until all have either folded or called. A third card is then dealt to all the players who have stayed. Again, the player with the highest upcards bets first, but now he may be showing a Pair, rather than just a high card. Also, he may check on the third card, instead of betting.

In that case, succeeding players may also check or bet. If he bets, they may either call, raise or fold. After all have called or folded, a fourth card is dealt to all who are still in the hand. The same procedure follows, but this time, it is possible for the high player to be showing Three of a Kind.

A fifth card is then dealt. Again, the player with the best upcards is the first to speak. After all bets are evened, the players who have stayed turn up their hole cards. The best hand wins. Often, competition is keen up to the fifth and final card.

Six Card Stud

This is a very remarkable outgrowth of Five Card Stud. Those who play Six Card Stud regularly regard it as the best of Poker games. They base this on the fact that interest fades in a Five Card game, when one hand is far too good in comparison with the other, which is often true.

So Six Card Stud was invented. It calls for the dealing of a sixth card, face down, which becomes an alternate card, replacing any card of the original five. There is an extra betting round on the sixth card, and with each player having two hole cards, the betting is apt to prove much stronger.

As a variation, some groups have the sixth card dealt as an upcard. This is a good game, too, but it tends to lessen the suspense, as five cards are actually showing, and might form a Straight, Flush or Full House, which would kill any other visible hand.

Seven Card Stud

This game, popularly known as Down the River and Seven Card Pete, has practically come to dominate the Stud situation. It is one step beyond the six card game, and puts the probabilities of Draw into Stud. This makes it the ideal form of Poker, in the estimate of many players. The procedure is as follows.

Three cards are dealt to each player. Two are downcards or hole cards. The third is an upcard and the players bet it exactly as in Five Card Stud. That constitutes the first betting round. The highest card showing—nearest to the dealer in case of a tie—must make a bet or fold.

A fourth card is dealt to each player. Now, the high hand can either check or bet. The same applies to a fifth card and a sixth, each being dealt face up. The seventh card is dealt face down, and another round of betting follows. After all the remaining players call, the hole cards are turned up and the player showing the best five cards wins.

To recap. Rounds of betting follow the deal of the 3rd, 4th, 5th, 6th and 7th cards. At the finish, three cards are down and four are up. Thus the players do not show their complete five card hands until all bets are called.

There is one important point to remember. In Draw or Five Card Stud, the hands are self-evident and must be judged accordingly. But in Seven Card Stud, they go according to the player's own declaration. If he holds a hand such as: K♠, Q♦, J♦, 10♥, 9♦, 5♦, 3♦ he might call it a King-high Straight—K, Q, J, 10, 9—by discarding the 5♦ and 3♦. But he would do better to call it a Diamond Flush—♦:Q,J,9,5,3—and throw out the K♠ and 10♥.

Eight Card Stud

Just like Seven Card Stud, but an eighth card is dealt face down and there is an additional betting round. With four downcards, it is much more difficult to guess the contents of another player's hand. More care must be taken in declaring hands, as more combinations are possible.

Since each player is able to reject three odd cards instead of only two, the hands hit a higher average than in Seven Card Stud, but the game is still sufficiently controlled to be regarded as sound Poker.

There are two options with Eight Card Stud.

1. Deal the 7th card face up and the 8th face down, or vice versa.

2. Deal the 7th and 8th cards together, so both are bet on the same round.

Nine and Ten Card Stud

These call for additional cards, resulting in hands that are too freakish for regular Poker play. The number of downcards and how they should be dealt for betting rounds should be decided upon beforehand.

In all forms of stud, if cards run short because of too many players, cards from folded hands are shuffled and used.

Stud Variations

Stud variations are numerous and are played under different names. In Five Card Stud, a round of betting may be made after dealing the hole cards. In some Stud games, players can turn up a hole card and take the next face down. In Seven Card Stud, all upcards can be dealt in the center, belonging to all hands, so that more players can be in the game.

Lowball

This is a development of Low Hand Poker in which the lowest hand wins. In its original form hands rank exactly as in regular Draw or Stud, but are valued in reverse, so that 7, 5, 4, 3, 2 of mixed suits is the best possible hand, and ♦: A,K,Q,J,10 is the worst. In Draw, players throw away high cards or Pairs hoping to catch low ones; while in Stud, the hand with the lowest card or cards showing is the hand that bets first.

Players may agree to count an Ace as low instead of high, so in that case—6, 4, 3, 2, A becomes the best possible hand. This is a logical addition, as high cards have no value. Thus the highest No Pair hand would be K, Q, J, 10, 9 of mixed suits. In the case of Pairs, the lower wins, the best being A, A, 2, 3, 4 with Ace low.

Lowball, in its most developed form, has gone beyond that. It is generally played as a form of Draw Poker, Straights and Flushes being ruled out entirely. Thus 5, 4, 3, 2, A becomes the best hand, regardless of suits, and is called a *Wheel*.

Chance of catching such a hand on the deal is about 1 out of 2500, so a Wheel is a trophy indeed, and worth going after on a draw. In Lowball, a player may still win with a fairly good draw. If holding K, 4, 3, 2, A he could discard the King, hoping to catch a Five; yet a Six, Seven or even an Eight would keep him in the action.

Anything opens in Lowball, since players are going for low not high. The game is played extensively in western gambling casinos, which often set their own special rules.

High Low Poker

A very popular form of Poker that may be played with almost any type of game. The play is as usual, but when the hands are finally declared, the player with the highest hand splits the pot with the one who holds the lowest.

Hands are rated as in standard Poker, hence the lowest card in a hand would normally be 7, 5, 4, 3, 2 of more than one suit. The highest card in the hand determines its value and a Seven is the lowest *high card* that a player can hold, as a hand running 6, 5, 4, 3, 2 would be a Straight.

In Draw Poker, players can stay on anything in High Low, so it is often hard to tell if a player is drawing for *high* or *low*, especially when he draws just one card. Pat hands, too, can be foolers.

In *Seven Card High Low*, the upcards are also deceptive and a player can vary his choice of final five cards to make up a high or low hand as he prefers. The same applies to *Six* or *Eight Card High Low*.

Originally, players each announced their best high or low and the pot was therewith split. Today, in most games, they must declare whether they are going after high or low. The one with the best hand in each department is the winner, but no one can switch after declaring.

Odd situations can arise with this rule. In Draw with High Low, A might go for high with 6, 6, 6, K, 8 and B might go for high with J, J, 7, 7, 5. A third player, C, holding Q, Q, 10, 10, 9 might figure that either A or B had a better high than his, so C would go for low.

In the showdown, A's three Sixes would beat B's Jacks Up for high. With B thus eliminated, C's Queens Up would be good for low, even though B held a lower Two Pair. Chances like this often encourage several players to stay in hope of *backing in* on either high or low, thus getting half the pot.

In *Seven Card High Low*, a player with ♦: **K,9,7,4,2**, ♠: **8,5** would have a King-high Diamond Flush for high, and an 8, 7, 5, 4, 2 for low, so he would have to use smart judgment to know which way to go. He might be beaten for high by a Full House, or for low by a hand headed by 8 and 6.

Nowadays, to make it still more exciting, in many games, a player is allowed to go for high *and* low. This means he is after both and if he wins them, he gets the whole pot. But if he loses either one, he loses both. The hand just given is the sort with which a player would go for *high and low*.

The best way to declare for high or low, is for each player to have a chip hidden in his fist. All are opened at once and anyone with a blue chip reveals that he is going for high; with a white chip, low. Where high and low is allowable, a player holds a red chip. Other types of markers can be used instead.

Or players can simply state high, low, or both, beginning with the first player to the dealer's left and going around the circle, including all players still in the hand.

Ace as High or Low is played a great deal nowadays. A player with a Flush would call his Ace a high card, but going for low, he would call an Ace low. With that rule, the lowest possible hand is 6, 4, 3, 2, A.

Dealer's Choice

The term *Dealer's Choice* applies to Poker games in which the dealer can name the type of game to be played during that hand. This may be limited to those already described and in some cases, a few of those—Eight or Nine Card Stud—may be disallowed. But in many social circles where the play is for small limits, Dealer's Choice may include a great variety of *wild* games, often with no restrictions whatever. Some of these are far removed from standard Poker, but many people regard them as fun. These games include the following.

Joker Wild

Joker Wild is the most reserved of wild games, in which a Joker is simply added to the pack and may represent any card that the holder names. Thus the highest hand becomes Five of a Kind, as a player holding Four Aces can call the Joker a fifth Ace of any suit. This takes precedence over a Royal Flush.

As part of an Ace-high Flush, a Joker can also represent a duplicate Ace, making his hand higher than a rival Ace-high Flush. Most often, the Joker is used to fill a hand like a Full House, or a Straight. The Joker, with a Pair, makes Three of a Kind; with Three of a Kind, it gives the player Four of a Kind.

Sometimes the use of the Joker is restricted to Ace, Straights or Flushes, but the modern trend is to make it completely wild. Two Jokers may be included in the pack, making the game *Double Joker Wild*.

Deuces Wild

Deuces Wild is played with the regular 52-card pack, the Deuces become wild, representing any card of any suit. In this game, Five of a Kind is the highest hand, followed by a Royal Flush and so on down. In case of *ties*, it may be agreed that a *natural* hand takes precedence, so that a Straight consisting of J♥, 10♠, 9♥, 8♠, 7♥ would beat out one composed of J♦, 2♠, 9♣, 8♣, 7♠. However, with a game being wild any embellishments may be added.

Deuces and 1-Eyed Jacks Wild

Deuces and One-Eyed Jacks Wild includes the J♥ and J♠ as wild cards, since their profiles show only one eye. The one-eyed King, which is the K♦ may be added as a wild card. One or two Jokers may be added to the pack as extra wild cards.

The dealer may specify any wild cards he wants, as Nines Wild or Sevens and Eights Wild. Sometimes a dealer may name an entire suit wild, so the game becomes Hearts Wild. One general rule is that when a player shows his hand, he must name it.

In Deuces Wild, a player holding 2♠, 2♣, A♦, J♥, 10♠ might call it Three Aces, but actually it can be rated as an A, K, Q, J, 10 Straight. In standard Poker, the hand *speaks for itself*, but not so in wild games. This is particularly important in games like *Seven Card Stud*, where players have to call their hands anyway.

Low Hole Card Wild

This game is a variant of *Seven Card Stud*, which is very exciting. Every player has a wild card, because when he turns up his hole cards, the lowest he holds makes others of that value wild. Thus with a 4♥ in the hole a player would have two wild cards if he had the 4♠ showing.

But if he should be dealt a 3♦ as his final hole card, his Fours would no longer be wild. Often, a player with a doubtful hand gets a break the other way about, on his final card.

Spit in the Ocean

Spit in the Ocean is a real wild game, with four cards dealt to each player and a fifth card dealt face up in the center of the table as a wild card belonging to everybody's hand. As usually played, all cards of that value are also wild. If the 10♦ turns up in the center and a player holds the 10♣, 10♠, K♥, 6♠ he automatically has Four Kings. Spit in the ocean is usually played as a form of Draw Poker.

However, the draw may be omitted, or the game can be played like *Five Card Stud* with the center card being turned up last, so no one knows what's wild until then.

Lame Brains

Lame Brains is like *Spit in the Ocean* but with this difference. Five cards are dealt to each player; then five are dealt face up one by one, in the center, with players betting on each, as in Stud. At the finish, each player makes up a five-card hand from those he holds and the cards showing on the table, those cards belonging to everybody's hand, as needed.

The lowest card of the five may also be declared wild, making all cards of its value wild. Suppose 7♦, J♥, 9♣, K♠ are up in the center, all Sevens are wild; but if the 5♣ turns up next, all Fives are wild instead.

In different versions, this game is known as *Around the World* and *Cincinnati*. In one form, only four cards are dealt to each player with four face up in the center. In another type, called *Crossover,* or *Criss-Cross,* the five cards are dealt face up in the center forming into a cross, and a player can only use one row of three as part of his hand. The center card is turned up last and is a wild card, making all of its value wild.

Baseball Poker

Baseball Poker is like *Seven Card Stud,* but with wild cards based on baseball rules. All Nines are wild, representing nine innings. All Threes are wild, but if one is dealt as an upcard, the player is *out* on three strikes, unless he pays a required number of chips into the pot. This is sometimes set as the amount already in the pot. A Four dealt face up is a walk and the player is dealt another card free. This can be face up or face down as agreed.

Football Poker

Football Poker is like *Baseball Poker*, but with a different set of wild cards. One way is to call Sixes wild, because a touchdown is six points. Deuces are wild, but one dealt face up is a *safety* and the player must drop out or pay up. A Three dealt face up is a field goal and the player is dealt an extra card.

Optional Card Poker

Optional Card Poker is played like *Six* or *Seven Card Stud*. After the *last* card is dealt, each player has the option of buying another card by putting a certain amount in the pot. Such optional cards may be dealt up or down as decided in advance.

Push Poker

Push Poker is like *Stud*, but if a player doesn't like a card dealt to him, he pushes it along to the next. If that player doesn't want it, he pushes it along, and so on. The dealer simply discards any card he doesn't want and takes another instead. At the finish, each player has the option of discarding a hole card and taking another. This, too, has variations.

Four Card Poker

Four Card Poker is played like *Stud* with one hole card, or like Draw with all cards down. Hands rank: Four of a Kind, Straight Flush, Straight, Three of a Kind, Two Pairs, Pair, Ace-high.

Three Card Poker

Three Card Poker is similar to *Four Card Poker*, with hands ranking: Straight Flush, Three of a Kind, Flush, Straight, Pair, or failing that, high card.

Two Card Poker

Two Card Poker follows the pattern of *Three* and *Four Card Poker*, but with players going simply for a Pair, or failing that, high card.

One Card Poker

One Card Poker is merely *High Card Wins* but with the lone card face down in *Stud*, so no one knows what the other bets.

RED DOG

A fast-moving betting game that can accommodate as many as ten players. Each contributes the same amount to a central pot, so seven players at 2 units each would make a pot of 14 units. Four cards are then dealt face down to each player.

Beginning at the dealer's left, each player bets that one of his cards can beat the next card to be dealt. Cards rank in the usual order: Ace, King, Queen down to Two, but the player's card must be of the same suit as the one he is to beat.

Thus, a player holding A♠, Q♦, 5♦, 10♣ can beat any Spade, any Diamond below the Queen, any Club below the Ten, but will be beaten by any Heart, since he has none.

The amount bet can be anything from a single unit up to the entire pot. With a poor holding, a player would bet the minimum; with anything approaching a sure hand of Four Aces, he would go for the pot; but many bets are somewhere in between.

A card is dealt face up, and if the player beats it, he collects the amount bet; if he loses, he puts that many chips into the pot. Play then moves to the next player, who bets against a new card to be dealt, and so on. Any time a player wins the pot, all players must contribute to a new pot.

Sometimes a series of heavy losses will cause the pot to grow to huge proportions. Hence in many games, particularly those with less than 7 or 8 players, five cards are dealt to each player, giving a better chance of winning than with only four.

RUMMY

One of the simplest as well as the most popular of card games. From it have stemmed more complicated and perhaps more sophisticated forms, all of which are understandable by anyone who has played the basic game. So our description will begin with standard Rummy, or Rum, as it is sometimes termed.

A 52-card pack is used, and cards are ranked from King down to Ace, in the order K, Q, J, 10, 9, 8, 7, 6, 5, 4, 3, 2, A. With two players, which is the ideal game, ten cards are dealt to each. With three or four players, each receives seven cards; beyond that each gets five or six. When the deal is completed, the top card of the pack is turned face up and laid beside the pack proper, which remains face down.

The first player to the dealer's left may then draw the top card from the pack, or pick up the face up card adding it to his hand. His object is to form groups consisting of three or four cards of the same value, as Q, Q, Q or 9, 9, 9, 9 or else to make a run of three or more cards in a single suit, as ♥: 3,2,A or ♦: J,10,9,8,7.

If he does that, he can lay down such a combination, face up. After that, he must discard from his hand, putting an odd card face up on the discard pile. The next player proceeds in the same manner, and play continues thus, with the following proviso:

Once a player has laid down a group of cards, another player may lay off on that group. Thus, if Player A should lay down 10, 10, 10; Player B could add another Ten. Or if A should lay down ♥: 8,7,6; B could *lay off* ♥: 5,4 so the run would be ♥: 8,7,6,5,4.

Often, a player can neither lay down nor lay off cards, but the draw may improve his hand, giving him future possibilities. Or, he may get rid of certain cards he does not want, by discarding them one by one.

The first player to lay down, lay off and discard his entire hand is the winner of that round. Other players must then show their remaining cards and the winner collects or gains points according to their value: Kings, Queens, Jacks counting 10 each; the rest, the number of their spots: 10, 9, 8 down to Ace for 1.

Thus if Player A clears his hand and Player B is left with J♦, 10♦, 3♥, 3♠; Player A would gain 26 points. With three or more players, the winner collects from all the rest according to their individual holdings. Game can be set at a fixed limit, as 50 points.

It should be decided, before the game, whether or not play should continue once the pack is used up. If agreed, the discard pile can be turned face down and play continued. In most games, it is agreed that if a player holds back his cards, instead of laying them down, or *melding* as it is also termed, he collects double if he can clear his hand all at once. This is called *going rummy* and in attempting it, the player runs the risk of getting *caught* if somebody else melds out ahead of him. Then he is stuck with what he holds.

That's all there is to Rummy, as the game was played for many years, but now it has new developments, which will be described under their respective heads.

Knock Rummy

Knock Rummy is exactly like the basic game, but players are not allowed to lay off on other hands. Instead, each player has the privilege of *knocking* on the table, whenever he wishes. Play halts immediately and each player lays down, or melds whatever he can, still without laying off on other hands.

If the cards still held by the knocker are less than those of other players, he collects the difference in count from each player. However, if the lowest player ties the knocker, the lowest player collects from the others, and the knocker is ruled out.

If the lowest player is lower than the knocker, he collects from all the rest, according to the difference in scores, and gets an extra 10 points from the knocker.

The game may be played on a chip basis, the knocker, if winner, collecting 1 chip from each opponent. If another ties the knocker or is lower, he collects instead, and the knocker must give him 2 chips.

Should the pack be down to a card for each player, the next draw is called the *break*. Draws continue and if no one *goes rum*, hands are shown and the player with the lowest count wins. If two tie, the one nearest the *break* wins; though in some circles, the farthest is the winner.

A player who knocks and goes rummy all at once gets 25 points from each opponent; or, in the *chip* game, he collects 3 chips from each.

Gin Rummy

Gin Rummy is a two-handed form of Rummy which rates as a distinctive game, but follows the basic pattern. Cards are dealt as described, ten to each player, but the first player must draw the upturned card, or let the dealer do so. If the dealer refuses, the first player draws the top card of the pack and play follows as in Knock Rummy, but with the following rule.

A player cannot knock until he has formed sufficient groups to bring his count of unmatched or non-meldable cards to as low as 10 points, allowing for his discard. He is not forced to knock then, but can go still lower if he wishes. As in Knock Rummy, the other player then lays down his combinations, but in Gin, he can lay off on the knocker's cards, giving him a special advantage.

Player A knocks and lays down the following.

♥: 8,7,6,5   6♦, 6♣, 6♠   5♦   2♣   A♣

His odd cards—5♦, 2♣, A♣—total 8 points. Player B might then lay down the following.

Q♣, Q♦, Q♥   ♠: 4,3,2   10♦, 10♥   9♥, 9♦

B's two groups Q, Q, Q and ♠: 4,3,2 are meldable on their own. Ordinarily, he might be stuck with two Tens and two Nines, for a total of 38 points. But here, he can lay off the 10♥ and 9♥ to form a top to A's run, making it ♥: 10,9,8, 7, 6,5. So B is caught only with the 10♦ and 9♦, a total of 19, which is 11 more than A's 8. This gives A a winning margin of 11.

Special scoring is used in Gin and it works in a cumulative fashion, with 100 points for game; the winner is also given any points over that. With each hand, he scores his margin —11, in the sample—against the other player's 0. However, if the other player cuts his hand down to the knocker's total or less, he scores a bonus of 25 points along with the winning margin.

In the sample shown, if B had been left with 2♥ and 2♦ instead of ♦: 10,9 B's count would have been 4, as against A's 8. So B wins and scores 29, 25 and 4.

If a player can lay down his entire hand in combinations J♥, J♦, J♣ ♥: 5,4,3,2 ♣: 3,2,A—he *goes Gin* and the other player cannot lay off on the knocker's hand. In addition, the knocker gets a 25 point bonus for Gin; the opponent cannot possibly meld out inasmuch as he is not allowed to *lay off*.

The player who wins the game receives a bonus of 100 points. Each player then is given 25 points for each hand he won during the game; this is called a box or line score, as it is added on after the game. In a close game, the loser may win more hands than the winner of the game; hence he may pile up enough *boxes* at 25 points each to creep up on the winner's 100 point bonus for game.

However, if the loser fails to win any hands at all, the winner doubles his score for *shutting out* his foe, and that represents the margin of victory, or *payoff*. Otherwise, the loser's total is subtracted from the winner's to find the winning margin.

Oklahoma Gin

In this stepped-up form of Gin Rummy, the value on the original face-up card sets the limit at which a player can knock. A face card or Ten keeps it at 10, as in regular Gin, but a Seven would make 7 the knock level; and so on down to Ace for 1.

By agreement, the knocker can be forced to *go Gin* if an Ace turns up. Another rule often included is to double all points if a Spade turns up on the deal. This applies only to

regular points in that hand. Otherwise, the laws of Gin
Rummy apply.

Hollywood Gin

This is strictly a scoring system that puts pep in Gin. Players use three score sheets: *Games 1, 2, 3.* A regular score is
kept with *Game 1,* until it is completed.

Upon winning his second hand, a player also scores it on
the sheet for *Game 2,* and he does the same with each succeeding win, until *Game 2* is completed. Upon winning his
third hand, a player also scores it on the sheet for *Game 3,*
and continues until that game is done.

Thus three games are being played simultaneously, but
they differ in totals, because each new game starts later than
the one before, and they run out one by one, until only the
final game is being scored. Hollywood Gin can be played on
a multiple scale, with more than three games, the number
being determined by agreement.

Around the Corner Rum

Applicable to regular Rum or Gin, this game has one special playing feature: an Ace can be regarded as either high or
low. Along with a sequence 3, 2, A a player may also form
A, K, Q or even a run like 2, A, K, Q provided all are the
same suit. If caught with an unmatched Ace, it costs the loser
5 points instead of only 1.

Five Hundred Rummy

An outgrowth of an earlier game called *Michigan Rummy,*
this is played by two or more persons and starts like regular

Rummy. When two people play, 13 cards are dealt to each. When more than two play, seven cards are dealt to each player. When more than five people play, two decks of cards are used. But as cards are laid on the face up discard pile, they are spread so all can be seen. Whenever a player sees a buried *discard* that he can use in an immediate lay down, or meld, he can pick it up; but he must also take up all the face up cards above it, that is, those that were discarded later than the wanted card.

Players lay down the usual combinations and they may also lay off on those already melded by other players; but each player keeps all his cards in front of him.

Once a player clears his hands and announces *Rummy*, he counts all his melded cards—lay downs and lay offs—according to the usual values, except that Aces in a group count 15 each, but only the usual 1 in a run like ♠: 3,2,A. That gives him his total for the hand. So a hand like K, K, K 10, 9, 8, 7, 6 3, 3, 3, 3 9, 8 5, 4 A Q would total 125. (The 9,8; 5,4; A; Q represent cards that were *laid off*.)

Other players add their melds, but must deduct any cards they still hold. If a player making the above meld was *caught* with J, J, 8, 4, 4, 2 he would have to subtract 38 from his 125, leaving him a total of 87. Sometimes, a player may be stuck with a minus score.

In any case, each total is added to the individual player's column and the one to reach 500 first is winner.

Michigan Rummy

In Michigan Rummy, the scoring is different. Each player' meld is recorded as he makes it. When one announce *Rummy*, others show their hands and he adds the total o their cards to his hand. The first player to reach 500 wins th game.

Pinochle Rummy

Pinochle Rummy is another name for *Five Hundred Rummy*.

SHEEPSHEAD

This is played like Skat, usually with four players, those seated opposite being partners. A 32-card pack is used and eight cards are dealt to each, with no skat or widow. Players bid for the privilege of naming a trump suit, running J♣, J♠ J♥, J♦ followed by A, 10, K, Q, 9, 8, 7 of the suit named. The sole object is to take counters—A:11, 10:10, K:4, Q:3, J:2—as in Skat, but there is no scoring beyond that.

Bidding starts at dealer's left. Each player may *Pass* or bid by fives, with 60 as the basis. A bid of *Five means 65; Ten, 70; Fifteen, 75;* and so on. In usual play, only one bid is allowed per person, and if nobody bids, the player holding the J♣ names trump.

Play begins on dealer's left and proceeds as in Skat. Partners combine their tricks and count cards are added at the finish of the hand. If a team makes its bid or better, it collects a specified number of chips. For 91 points, they win double; for 120, triple or four times—if so agreed.

If a bidding team fails to make 61 points, it loses the specified chips; if it fails to make 31 points, it loses double; if it fails to take any tricks, it loses triple or four times—if agreed.

The game can be played three-handed, with a two-card skat which goes to the bidder, who takes it into his hand and discards two cards. The discards go with his tricks; and he wins or loses points instead of chips, on a basis of 1, 2, 3 per hand. Game is set at 5 or 10 points as preferred.

More punch may be added to Sheepshead by making the Black Queens top trump—Q♣ then the Q♠—above the four Jacks. It becomes still stronger when all four Queens are trumps, which then run as follows.

Q♣,Q♠,Q♥,Q♦   J♣,J♠,J♥,J♦   A,10,K,9,8,7 of trump

SIX BID SOLO

So called to distinguish it from *Solo* as played in Skat, this fast-moving game requires a 36-card pack, values running A, 10, K, Q, J, 9, 8, 7, 6. One suit is named trump, except in Nullo, and certain cards taken in play count for points, as Aces: 11, Tens: 10, Kings: 4, Queens: 3, Jacks: 2.

Eleven cards are dealt to each of three players, with three laid aside as a widow. The widow never figures into play, but goes to the bidder at the end of a trump hand; and is disregarded when Nullo is declared. Since bidding precedes play, it will be described first. Bidding begins at the dealer's left and there are six fixed bids, ascending in order.

SOLO. The player names any trump except Hearts. He must win 60 points. For each point over 60, he collects 2 chips from each opponent. For each point under 60, he pays 2 chips to each.

HEART SOLO: The bidder must make Hearts trump. He collects 3 chips for each point over 60; pays 3 for each point under.

134

NULLO. The bidder must avoid taking any counters. If successful, he wins 30 chips; if he fails, he pays out 30 chips.

GUARANTEE. Like Solo, but the bidder must take 74 points if he names Hearts trump; or 80 points if he names another suit. He wins or loses 40 chips in either case.

SPREAD NULLO. This is simply Nullo, with a slight variation, but the bidder must spread his hand face up, giving the other players an advantage in their leads. He wins or loses 60 chips.

CALL SOLO. Here, the bidder must win all the counters; or, if so agreed, he must take every trick. However, before naming trump, he is allowed to *call* for any card he wants, and the player holding it must hand it over, the bidder giving him a card in return. If the called card is in the widow, it stays there, going along with the bidder's tricks. With Call Solo, the bidder wins or loses 100 chips; or 150 if he names Hearts trump.

Play normally begins with the player at the dealer's left, regardless of who made the bid. Player may lead any card he chooses; the other two must follow suit if possible. *If out of suit, a player must trump,* but he does not have to play a higher trump. If he has no trump, he may discard. Winner of a trick leads to the next.

In Nullo, there is no trump, so it is just a case of following suit or discarding when out. Play starts at dealer's left, except in a Spread Nullo, when it begins at bidder's left.

Four players frequently make up a Solo session, with each acting as the dealer, in turn. Like the two non-bidders, the dealer pays or receives the specified number of chips, according to whether the bidder wins or loses. Score may be kept instead of using chips.

Six Bid Solo stems from an earlier game called *Frog* which in turn comes from *Skat*. Hence there are several varieties of Solo, and the game's popularity in the American West resulted in different local rules. In some circles, a player is not forced to trump when out of suit, but can discard instead. Hence, rules should be discussed and agreed upon beforehand.

SKAT

This game is played with a pack of 32 cards, Aces down to Sevens, but with special rankings, as will be described. There are three active players, who can be termed A, B, C for convenience, with a fourth, D, serving as dealer. The second deal is made by A, with D an active player; then B, and so on around. With only three players, A, B, C each deals in turn.

Ten cards are dealt to each player, usually by threes, with one round of four, and in between, two cards are dealt face down, to form a special group, or *skat*. Players then bid for the privilege of naming the type of game to be played during that hand, as there are several varieties of Skat. To simplify these, each game will be described individually.

Tournee

In this game, the bidder turns up the top card of the skat to name a trump suit; if he does not like that card, he turns up the other for trump, but this doubles his risk during the play that follows. The four Jacks are *always* the top cards in trump, and they run **J♣, J♠, J♥, J♦** followed by A, 10, K, Q, 9, 8, 7 of the suit named. Other suits run A, 10, K, Q, 9, 8, 7.

The lead is made by the first player to the dealer's left, in this case, A, whether or not he is bidder. Others must follow suit if they can, otherwise, a player may trump. The highest card of the suit, or trump, takes the trick; and that player leads to next.

The purpose is to take cards with certain count values, namely Aces:11, Tens:10, Kings:4, Queens:3, Jacks:2. These add up to 120, so to make game in Tournee, the bidder needs 61 points. He is allowed to add the skat cards to his hand and discard two others, which count toward his total score, being added to whatever tricks he takes.

Making game in Tournee gives the bidder 1 unit. If he gathers 91 points, his opponents are *Schneidered* and he gets 2 units. If he takes all the tricks, they are *schwartzed* and he gets 3 units. These apply in reverse as will be described.

Solo

In this game, the bidder names the suit he wants for trump and plays without looking at the skat, which is added to his tricks at the end of the hand, so its cards are included in his count toward game.

Trump suit is headed by the **J♣, J♠, J♥, J♦** with the named suit following A, 10, K, Q, 9, 8, 7 as in Tournee. The purpose is also the same: to take cards with count values as already specified. He gets 1 unit for *game*, 2 if he *Schneiders* his opponents, 3 if he *Schwartzes* them. But in Solo, he is allowed to declare Schneider or Schwartz before play begins.

For Schneider declared and made, he gets 3 units instead of just 2. If he declares Schneider and makes Schwartz, he

THE KEY TO HOYLE'S GAMES

gets 4 units. If he declares Schwartz and makes it, he gets 5 units. Hence with a very strong hand, a player frequently elects to play Solo, in order to go for the extra units.

Grand

In this game, the four Jacks form a trump suit of their own, in the usual order J♣, J♠, J♥, J♦. The other four suits run A, 10, K, Q, 9, 8, 7. So there are really five suits. The Grand games are of different types.

Tournee Grand

Like Tournee, but if the bidder turns up a Jack in the skat, he can name Jacks as trump instead of the suit, and play the hand with a chance for a bigger score than in plain Tournee.

Gucki Grand

Instead of turning up a card from the skat, the bidder announces *Gucki Grand* which gives him a chance for a bigger score than Tournee Grand. He then adds the skat cards to his hand and discards any two he does not want. Losing at Gucki Grand costs the bidder double.

Solo Grand

The same game as Solo, but the bidder names Jacks as trump and plays without looking at the skat. A higher score can be made in Solo Grand than in ordinary Solo.

Open Grand

Also known as *Grand Ouvert*, this game demands that the bidder play Solo Grand, but with his hand face up on the table, excluding the skat. He must also take all the tricks, so Open Grand automatically includes *Schwartz* announced.

Nullo

In contrast to Open Grand, which demands a very strong hand, Nullo may be played with a very weak hand. There is no trump in Nullo and the cards rank in the conventional order of A, K, Q, J, 10, 9, 8, 7. The whole purpose is for the bidder to lose every trick. Hence there are no counter cards in Nullo.

Open Nullo

Open Nullo or *Nullo Ouvert* can be played with cards face up, at double risk.

Scoring in Skat

From the descriptions so far given, Skat is a simple game, or rather, a group of simple games, according to which the bidder wants to play. Since the bidding depends on the scoring, it is preferable to outline the scoring system first. It depends upon unit values, beginning with *Game* as 1, and including *Schneider* and *Schwartz*, when they occur. To these are added other units called *Matadores*. The total number of units is then multiplied by specific values given to the trump suits, according to the particular form of Skat that the bidder decides to play.

Matadores are simply trumps in sequence, beginning from the top down. Thus, if the bidder holds the J♣, but not the J♠, he is playing the hand *with* one Matadore. If he held the J♣, J♠, J♥ but not the J♦, he would be playing *with* three Matadores. If a bidder held all four Jacks and the Ace, Ten and King of Hearts, he could declare Hearts trump and would be playing *with* seven Matadores. It is possible for the bidder to play *with* eleven Matadores—J♣, J♠, J♥, J♦ ♥: A,10,K,Q,9,8,7—because he could have ten in his hand and one in the skat, which belongs to him.

But the bidder must remember that any break in the descending sequence limits the Matadores to those above. Also, in Grand games, where Jacks alone are trumps, four is the greatest number of possible Matadores.

Matadores also count as units for the bidder if he is *without* them. If he lacks the J♣, but has the J♠, he is playing *without* one Matadore. If he has no Jacks, he is *without* four Matadores, which would be his limit in a Grand bid; but if his highest Heart was the King, he could name Hearts trump and play without trumps—♥: K,Q,9,8,7—if he hoped to make enough count for Game, which is essential.

The bidder must remember that Game is the vital unit; or he loses the hand. Also, when playing *without* Matadores, the skat becomes a risk. Holding the J♦ as his highest card, the bidder may *think* he was playing *without* three Matadores. But if the J♣ showed up in the skat, he would be playing *with* only one.

In every hand, there is *one unit* that the bidder must make, Game. He is also sure of *one unit* for a Matadore, *with* or *without*. So he figures his units from two on up. If he held the four Jacks and all the Hearts down to the 7♥, his Game unit would stretch to 5, because he would be sure of a declared Schwartz; and his Matadores would give him 10 units, not risking the chance of the 11th being in the skat, so he would have 15 units in all. But most hands promise a number of units somewhere in between, particularly when playing *without* Matadores.

Having estimated his potential units, the bidder now considers multipliers, according to the following schedule.

TOURNEE

♦ trump 5	♥ trump 6	♠ trump 7	♣ trump 8
♦ trump 9	♥ trump 10	♠ trump 11	♣ trump 12

TOURNEE GRAND 12	GUCKI GRAND 16
SOLO GRAND 20	NULLO 20
OPEN GRAND 24	OPEN NULLO 40

A minimum bid is 10 points and bids are generally kept at low levels, for although a bidder gets credit for all the points he makes, if he fails to reach Game—61 counters—he is set back the amount he bid. The same applies to Schneider and Schwartz. Also, if he fails to make the amount bid, he is set back accordingly. For instance, a player bids 60 and goes for a Diamond Solo at 63, 7 units multiplied by 9. If he fails to make it, he is set back 63, not just 60.

Consider the following sample hand.

J♣, J♠, J♥, J♦   ♥: A   ♣: 10,K   ♦: Q,9,7

Playing Solo with Diamonds trump, the bidder would probably lose only one trick—the K♣—so he can figure his hand as Game with Schneider declared, 3 units, with four Matadores, 4 units, making 7 multiplied by 9 for 63.

Playing Solo with Hearts trump, he should take six tricks, but Schneider is doubtful. Figure 1 for Game, 5 for five Matadores, including A♥, making 6 units multiplied by 10 for 60, a proper bid. If he makes Schneider, he will score 70.

Playing Grand Solo, with Jacks trump, figure Game for 1 unit, four Matadores, 4, making 5 units, multiplied by 20 for

Solo Grand, giving a total of 100, as a still better bid and play.

Bidding follows a special pattern in Skat. The first player to the dealer's left, called *Vorhand*, decides how high he will go, but does not state it. Instead, he lets the second player, *Mittelhand*, question him in bidding style: "Ten?" . . . "Twelve?" . . . "Fourteen?" . . . and so on, meaning that the second player will go that high if the first will let him. If the second player gives up, the third player, *Hinterhand*, can continue with such bids. If he quits, the first player gains the bid at the amount last stated by either the second or third.

In scoring, the bidder is credited with points won, while any loss is deducted from his score, which may run him into the minus column. Losses are doubled if he turned up a second card in Tournee or Tournee Grand, as well as Gucki Grand or Open Nullo.

If the bidder declares either Schneider or Schwartz and fails to make it, he loses just as if he failed to reach Game, even though he makes more points than he bid. If he fails to count 31 during play, he is Schneidered and loses an extra multiple; or if he fails to take a trick, he is Schwartzed and loses twice that. That is, what he could have gained by a Schneider or Schwartz, he loses, if either happens to him.

In informal play, Skat works on a time basis, at the end of a session, players settle according to their respective scores, rather than a fixed total.

In tournament play, Skat is subject to more exacting and detailed rules, under the jurisdiction of a *Skatmeister*, whose decision stands.

Otherwise, the game may be varied according to local rules, which have characterized the development of Skat from the early German game up to the modern American form.

Ramsch

When nobody bids, Jacks become trumps, as in Grand. The first player leads, and each is on his own, but his aim is to avoid counts. The regular rule applies; Aces:11, Tens:10, Kings:4, Queens:3, Jacks:2 but whoever takes the lowest total wins the hand.

Ramsch is the name of this game, and the winner is credited with 10 points. If he avoids taking any tricks at all, he wins 20 points. If one player is soaked with all the tricks, he loses 30 points. Sometimes the other two combine toward that aim.

SPOIL FIVE

An old and once highly popular game of the trick-taking type, with one suit declared trump, thereby gaining precedence over the others. The most striking feature of Spoil Five is the unique ranking of the values. This differs among the ordinary suits and when a suit becomes trump, it undergoes another change.

	Rank as Ordinary Suits
Spades	K, Q, J, A, 2, 3, 4, 5, 6, 7, 8, 9, 10
Clubs	K, Q, J, A, 2, 3, 4, 5, 6, 7, 8, 9, 10
Diamonds	K, Q, J, 10, 9, 8, 7, 6, 5, 4, 3, 2, A
Hearts	K, Q, J, 10, 9, 8, 7, 6, 5, 4, 3, 2

Note that King is high, followed by Queen, then Jack. The Ace is regarded as a spot card and the spots rank "from lowest up in Black" and "from highest down in Red." There is no Ace in the ordinary Heart suit, as the A♥ is *always* a trump—shown as follows.

TRUMP RANK OF SUIT

Spades	5, J A♥	Spades	A,K,Q,2,3,4,6,7,8,9,10
Clubs	5, J A♥	Clubs	A,K,Q,2,3,4,6,7,8,9,10
Diamonds	5, J A♥	Diamonds	A,K,Q,10,9,8,7,6,4,3,2
Hearts	5, J, A, K, Q, 10, 9, 8, 7, 6, 4, 3, 2		

The game is played two to ten players, each for himself. Each is dealt five cards, usually two or three at a time. The next card is turned face up on the pack to show the trump suit. The players look at their hands and anyone holding the Ace of trump takes the trump card from the pack, adds it to his hand and discards another card face down.

This is called *robbing the trump*, and in the original game it was a strict requirement, but later became an option. Since it is usually to a player's advantage to add the robbed trump to his hand, such an oversight would work against him. If the Ace of trump happens to be turned up on the pack, the dealer *robs* the Ace for his own hand, discarding some less valuable card face down.

The player at the dealer's left then leads any card he wishes. Others must follow suit unless they prefer to trump, which they can do at any time. If out of suit, they can either trump or throw a card from another suit. The highest card of the suit led takes the trick unless trumped; in that case the highest trump wins. The winner makes the next lead.

However, a special rule applies to the three top cards— Five of trump, Jack of trump and Ace of Hearts. When a trump is led, a player does not have to play one of the *big three* unless the lead is a higher trump.

For example, with Diamonds trump: Player A leads the K♦. Player B holding the A♥, and no other trump, can retain it for future use. But if A had led the 5♦ or the J♦, B would have had to play the A♥ and lose it.

This rule prevents *forcing out* one of the big three by a low trump lead; but two top cards still are able to *draw out* a lower trump of their own class.

In Spoil Five, each hand is like a game in itself. Before the deal, players contribute chips to a pool—say two chips each —and anyone winning these tricks takes the whole amount. If he takes all five tricks, he scores a *jink* and collects double, the other players each contributing the same amount that they placed in the pool.

Some groups go by the rule that when a player takes the first three tricks, he can call it quits and take the pool. But if he decides to go jink for double and fails to make it, the pool remains untaken. In short, his three tricks do not count.

In any hand where no individual player is able to take three or more tricks, the hand is *spoiled* and the pool remains. The deal moves to the next player and each player again contributes to the pool, which can grow to large proportions when several hands are *spoiled* in succession. The larger the group, the more apt this is to happen, the greater the contribution per hand.

Any player committing an infraction of a rule, such as robbing the trump without an Ace, or failing to follow suit when required, is counted out of that hand, and must contribute to successive pools without playing, until a pool is won.

Twenty-Five

Twenty-Five is a game identical with Spoil Five except that players score any tricks they make, and therefore no hands are *spoiled*. A hand is dealt and played as usual, each trick counting 5 points, and a total of 25 wins the game. This may require several deals, according to the number of players.

Four players may form two teams of two partners each, or six players may form three such teams, or two teams of three each. Partners are seated opposite, or alternately. There is no *jink*, as any team taking five tricks automatically wins the game.

Forty-Five

Forty-Five is an extension of Twenty-Five with 45 points required to win the game. To step up the scoring, some groups add the rule that anyone holding the highest trump in play scores an extra 5 points.

If two players are approaching the 45 total, tricks are counted before the high trick at the end of the hand, to determine which is winner. A *jink* is included in this game, but the player or team making it is simply credited with enough extra points to reach 45 and win the game. There is no bonus in the way of chips.

Variations have been introduced to both these games. Some modern players rank any trump suits *from highest down*, whether Red or Black, but follow the usual rule with ordinary suits.

WHIST

Once the most popular of card games, Whist is played with a 52-card pack, with cards ranking Ace, King, Queen, Jack, Ten on down to Two. There are four players, those facing each other being partners. Cards are dealt singly around the table to the left, the last card being turned face up to designate the trump suit, after which it is taken into the dealer's hand.

The player to the left of the dealer leads any card he wants. The others must follow suit, unless out of it; then he may trump or discard. The highest card of the suit led wins the trick; except when trumps are played, the highest trump always wins. The player taking a trick leads to the next until thirteen have been played.

Six tricks are a book, or the required minimum before a team can score. For each trick over book, a team scores a point. In American play, seven points represent game, hence a game can be won in a single hand, if a team makes a slam, by taking every trick. Usually, several hands are required before one team reaches seven points, the deal passing to the left with each new hand.

If both teams score points during the course of several hands, the margin of victory is determined by subtracting the losing team's score from seven.

In English play, the teams go for rubber, or the best of three games. A game is five points, and honors are counted along with tricks. Honors are the Ace, King, Queen, Jack of trumps, so a team holding all four scores 4 points; or holding three, 2 points; while two, being equally divided, scores 0. Tricks, however, are scored ahead of honors.

A game won by a score of 5 to 0 counts 3 points; by a score of 5 to 1 or 2, 2 points; by a score of 5 to 3 or 4, 1 point. Winning the rubber counts 2 points. If the losers have won a game, its score is deducted from the winner's score.

Thus, Team A might win the first game, 5 to 3, for 1 point; Team B, the second, 5 to 0, for 3 points; Team A, the third, 5 to 1, for 2 points, gaining 2 points for rubber. Team A has a total of 5 points, Team B, 3 points, so Team A wins by 2 points.

Whist stems from a game called *Ruffs and Honors,* and the term ruff is still used to denote the trumping process. Later forms of the game were *Cayenne* and *Boston,* which was popularized by Benjamin Franklin. In *Duplicate Whist,* players at different tables were dealt the same cards, to see which team could fare best in the play.

Bid Whist

Bid Whist involves bidding for the privilege of declaring trump, instead of turning up the last card dealt. Bidding begins at the dealer's left and continues around, each player raising the number of tricks and honors he and his partner must take in play to win the hand. The highest bid stands after the other three players all pass. That bidder then names the trump suit, and makes the first lead.

Since there are 13 tricks and 4 honors, the highest possible bid is 17. At the end of the hand, each team scores the points it made, but unless a team makes the amount bid, or more, it does not score. Thus if Team A bids Eleven and takes only eight tricks and two honors, it would score 0, while Team B would score 7, because it made five tricks and had two honors. It may also be agreed that a team must take a majority of the tricks to make its bid. Thus a team bidding Ten and taking six tricks and four honors would lose, being one trick short.

Hands are settled by deducting the lower score from the higher, to establish the margin of the win. If desired, winning points can be added hand by hand, the first team to reach 50 being the winner. Other modes of scoring may be used; in forms of play, honors are eliminated, and only tricks are counted.

French Whist

French Whist is similar to regular Whist, with the final card being turned up as trump, and play beginning at the dealer's left. Each trick over book counts 1 point, and each honor 1 point for the team taking it. The Ten of Diamonds also counts 10 points when taken, regardless of what suit is trump. Game is 40 points, won by the team that first reaches that score.

Scotch Whist

Scotch Whist, *Catch the Ten,* is played with a 36-card pack, trump suit running in value: Jack, Ace, King, Queen, Ten and down to Six. Ordinary suits go Ace down to Six as usual. There is no score for tricks and honors in the accepted sense. Instead, a team tries to *catch* the Ten of trump for 10 points, then to take the most cards, each card over eighteen counting 1 point, and to take the following trumps—Ace:4, King:3, Queen:2, Jack:11. The Jack, being the *highest trump*, is a sure count of 11 for the team holding it, so much of the strategy revolves about *catching the Ten* for its valuable 10 points.

Game is 41 points, all points being scored by both teams in each hand. It is possible to score 48 points with a slam, and teams can also score equally with 16 points each. Hence, when approaching 41, the points for the Ten should be counted first, followed by others in the order given, the first team reaching 41 becoming the winner.

Instead of a partnership game, Catch the Ten can be played by individual players, as few as three and as many as seven. Where there is an odd card, it is turned up to designate trump and is then thrown out of play. In scoring for *cards*, each player is given 1 point for every card above the number originally dealt to him.

Index

153